I0706855

CHEAP SHOTS

KAREN KELLOCK PH.D.

**Manual for
Superior Men**

**A complete theory based on Einstein physics,
Political Psychology, Systems Theory
and Archetypal Psychiatry.**

FORMULA

**All success attraction
All disease obstruction
All recovery elimination**

**You must fast on all three
OBSTRUCTIONS:
People
Habit
Food**

CHEAP SHOTS

When I repented God took out all my enemies: He was waiting for ME. The older I get the more terrifying it is to look back, I was dense to dangers in fact.   I don't know who's crueler, youth or older. The latter have more savvy to ruin you but youth are crazier too. The envious are so insidious they wish bad things happening to you or good taken away. Jezebel suppressed her envy but started criticizing while triangulating with the enemy. When someone envies you it's hate, not the "greatest form of flattery".   Cut your losses/move on to friends happy in your growth because they are whole.

CHEAP SHOTS

THE ENVIOUS ARE YOUR ENEMIES
OUTER DIRECTEDNESS OF NARCISSISTS
WOMEN BREAKING THRU THE HAZE
CRAZY MAL-ADAPTING TO LIBERAL THINKING
SOCIAL IS BOTHERING ME
MOST WOMEN ARE LIBERAL FEMINISTS
NARCS WANT YOU TO SUFFER
SLUTS POLITIX AND SIDEKICKS
SYSTEM DEVICES TO HURT YOU
GET YOU OUTA THE HOUSE
ABUSE BY PROXY
THE WEAK FIGHT THRU FLYING MONKEYS
FLYING MONKEYS ARE DUMB ENFORCERS
UNINVITED GROUPS ARE AN ATTACK!
SERIAL SISTER BETRAYALS
CALUMNY IS HIX POLITIX
GLOBALISTS/DEMOCRATS PUSH DESTRUCTION
PREDESTINATION/PLAN OF SALVATION
PATIENCE IS STRENGTH, SLOW TO ANGER
KINDNESS AND GOODNESS
FORGIVENESS
TONGUES DO NOT EDIFY
GIFTS ARE FOR EDIFYING MEN
DON'T CALL ME "FRIEND"
CHOOSE YOUR OWN INTERVIEWER
WHITE ANTI-WHITES ARE THE WORST

CHEAP SHOTS

WHEN I HEAR TRUE PREACHING
SOCIAL OR HEDGE OF PROTECTION?
I'M NOT ALL ONE WITH THAT!
PEACE AT ANY PRICE AIN'T EASIER
WOMEN ARE HOME CREATORS
BYE BYE OR BE DEAD
THEY DON'T MISS YOU LIKE A HUMAN
WITHOUT BOUNDARIES LIFE IS RUINED
THEY WILL TRIANGULATE WITH ANYONE
APPROVAL-GETTING IS VERY BORING
STIRRING YOUR EMOTIONS IS HIS SUPPLY
MOVE FORWARD, GO NO-CONTACT
NARCISSISM IS EVERYWHERE
CONTRIVED SURFACE PERSONALITIES
FIRM FOUNDATION OF IDENTITY
NARCISSIST IS TWO PEOPLE IN ONE
STOP GIVING UP YOUR PERSONALITY
REASONS ARE MEANINGLESS
NOT JUST THE TOWN SLUT ANYMORE
NARCISSISTS HAVE A SHORT FUSE
NARC HAREMS
RAPID CYCLING
FEMALE NARCISSISTS
NARC MOM JEALOUSIES
FORGIVING T DRAMA QUEENSHIP
NARC EXPOSURE WEARS YOU DOWN

CHEAP SHOTS

CHEAP SHOTS

LET HIM REMOVE THE STAIN/GIVE SECURITY
CHEAP SHOTS: ALCOHOL AND ANOSOGNOSIA
NO SOCIAL DRINKING FOR ALCOHOLICS
FOOD/ALCOHOL COMPULSIONS
NECESSARY DAY OF HUMILIATION
DEPRAVED MINDS
THO' THEY KNOW IT'S WRONG
LIVING LIFE AS HE WILT THE SPIRIT WILTS
FALSE RELIGION IS THE LOWEST
VISIBLE CYCLES IN HISTORY
GOAL: FIND YOUR NICHE/WILL MAKE YA RICH
IT'S ABOUT LOOSE FLESH
ENGINEERED VIRUS
STARCHIVORE-PESCATARIAN-FASTARIAN [ITALIAN]
IT'S EATING LIKE EUROPEANS
BAD DRIVERS ARE SELFISH
NEVER BORED NOR LONELY
TEMPERAMENTAL DIGESTION
Karen Kellock on Completion and the Creative Act
COMPLETION IS BACK TO CHILD
TWO LIVES: PREPARATION AND SUCCESS
A LADY HAS GRACE AND INTELLIGENCE
SICK OF IT: I JUST WANT JESUS
AVOID SELF-PROMOTION, YOU'RE ROTTEN
MAJOR PROBLEM: NOT STANDING GROUND
SELF-GLORIFICATION OR BE GLORIFIED?

CHEAP SHOTS

It's true: as soon as I repented God took out all my enemies. He was waiting for ME.

The older I get the more terrifying it is to look back. How dense I was to dangers which I denied in fact.

I don't know who's crueler, youth or older. The latter have more savvy to ruin you but youth are crazier too.

THE ENVIOUS ARE YOUR ENEMIES

The ENVIOUS are so insidious they actually wish bad things to happen to you or good taken away.

Stay away from envy. When someone envies you they hate your guts--it's not the "greatest form of flattery".

Be careful of the envious cuz they make you feel bad about yourself without knowing why. They are enemies.

Cut your losses and move on to a friend who can be happy in your growth because he/she is WHOLE.

Whenever someone pulls away because you're doing better it means they are ENVIOUS.

She held in her envy of me. But she started criticizing what I did and triangulating with the enemy.

Say to yourself: This person could be envious of me and it's NOTHING I've done nor any of my business.

If someone is envious of you/won't give credit where it's due then they hate you/they're the foe too.

These kids will do anything--they have no lines about a thing. Take it from me this was terrifying.

CHEAP SHOTS

It was obvious Jezebel didn't have any lines about a thing. It was frightening to anyone with any decency.

We have to draw lines between our business and the others. ENVY is their business tho' it hurts us.

One with high self-esteem knows he CAN do it and that he DOES deserve it. But his enviers thwart this.

They will tell you things like "you can't do it" or why it can't be done and why you don't deserve it.

Fame and fortune doesn't come from shaking hands in Boca Raton but hard WORK on your own man.

OUTER DIRECTEDNESS OF NARCISSISTS

It's by doing our WORK which was designed by God before our BIRTH. Not socializing like a buncha jerks.

Having been thrown crumbs the target becomes addicted to ever-lessening approval: a trauma-bond.

They're so good at it: "I've worked so hard at the relationship but I gotta tell you some things."

The narcissist is so good at this since he's wholly based on outer-directedness and you're less that way.

"I hate to be the one to bring it to you but I think you need to hear this". They are that good at this dis.

The narc is only motivated by POWER and he gets it by manipulating everyone to his side with you lower.

My first husband was so socially manipulative he managed to have flying monkey armies against me constantly.

He was a wino too and as happens with the wife of the alcoholic he blames/scapegoats her to the public.

CHEAP SHOTS

I'd think: how could he be so good at this? Turning everyone against me and I had no defense.

Being around people was such a stink I'd seek a drink.

WOMEN BREAKING THRU THE HAZE

Most women are dumb but those who make it thru the feminist haze become the greatest.

I've known many narcissists and what I've found is those who SEEM like one aren't--just like Trump.

So you're angry--what are you gonna do go yell and scream at someone in a rest home? Get over it.

If men don't think women hate women just as much, ask one with two older sisters where there was no love.

The internet can be even WORSE than TV yet you're so self-congratulatory as a nerd--yah, right...

No matter how crazy I was my parents are now eternally grateful I led em to Christ--the scripture says it.

It makes me so happy to know that no matter how crazy I was, if I led em to Christ they are eternally grateful.

Just the thought of that is such a relief, I always felt so embarrassed but now I see: they're in ETERNITY.

There's energy in the air, it's palpable, a time of great movement and transition and I am ABLE.

CRAZY MAL-ADAPTING TO LIBERAL THINKING

One can get crazy mal-adapting to liberal thinking and he ends up the worst of the lot unfortunately.

We must support our president. This is our country, he's making it great while the rest of the world is shitty.

CHEAP SHOTS

Anything wrong with our country, like the cities, is due to the demonrats who run it, failing intentionally.

I thank you for your continued patience. I can't rush destiny, things unfold on their own, that is best.

As women we were taught we were supposed to be furious. I was too before getting serious.

I lost my grant when I said I was a vessel. Hmmm--even though it went along with science also?

When I think of some of the people I attracted in earlier phases it makes me amazed--I was that crazy?

Forgive yourself for swimming in muddy waters and getting some of it on ya-- from insecurity, who could blame ya.

SOCIAL IS BOTHERING ME

What you call "socializing" I call "bothering me".

Far more edifying than hix politix is putting music on and watching my pets' interactions, fantastic.

He's beginning to show who he is. No matter what he does to compensate we all know/can sense it.

It's the careless ease of self-confident fools that destroys them. Prov 1: 32. So just wait, God'll get em.

The careless ease of self-confident fools arrogantly going on their way, making you their slave.

They were so arrogantly cruel and stupid as we licked their boots but that's over now, it's all reversed.

Because they were bored and lonely they'd never leave me alone--on top of that get mad at me as the throne.

CHEAP SHOTS

You rule your own domain but if weak or needing their approval they'll bring you down or drain.

I know it's inspired it's a matter of being **STRONG** enough to sustain it for long hours or days at a time.

Simply put, I need Your protection to continue my work alone but I'll make it well worth your while.

Well honey I gotta write whatever comes up. What do you expect me to do, make something up?

It just happened and there's not a thing anyone can do about it. That's attraction, love, acceptance.

The problem is their flying monkeys: that's when a frenemy gets an army against you, truly.

Making a traveling business hussie stay home just makes her open to neighbors etc. cuz she's never alone.

MOST WOMEN ARE LIBERAL FEMINISTS

MOST women today are liberal feminists---isn't that the problem, not women per se?

Homosexuality is part of the depopulation program and that's why they push it: what a scam.

They "look" better all made up as fantastical creatures and that lures the youth even the toddlers.

Mommy porn is worse than visual for a highly mental man cuz it opens up windows--make it taboo too.

Liberals have such dirty minds that if you love cats and dogs they assume you're having sex with em.

Yes, as I look back I went insane adapting to liberals and I lived to write about it, having figured it ALL out

CHEAP SHOTS

The problem isn't women, it's feminism--but unfortunately most are feminist by default, even in the pews.

Brad Pitt said he never watches his pictures and never reads the comments. That's the answer, amen!

Should we be cannibals since there's a tribe somewhere who eats humans? Dogs aren't food they're friends!

When you hear her say "don't hate" or "be nice" you know she's new age because Holy Hatred is divine.

Hope keeps expecting that today is the day. Joyce Meyer

Righteous aren't defeated by setbacks. No matter how many times you knock em down they're right back.

The most important thing ever is turning off the RINGER. It's off all the time or someone else will answer.

The dam ringer is just as bad as someone coming to the door. It's an INTERRUPTION--that's all that matters.

NARCS WANT YOU TO SUFFER

Narcissists want to destroy you by taking over your personal power--feeling good when you suffer.

It's rarely overt--the narc will abuse you in underhanded ways. Secretively, slyly, shrewdly they slay.

No matter how much I did for a woman I knew she'd SLAY me with her men who'd come after me.

This weak woman would find fawning men to do her bidding. A slut has many men in a secret army.

It came from her felt weakness vis-a-vis me and could have been subconscious in her psychology.

CHEAP SHOTS

Her sidekicks will do the bidding of the narcissist and abuse YOU as her surrogate: HIX POLITIX.

She'd brag about "doing it with everyone" and that was her power base in this liberal small town.

SLUTS POLITIX AND SIDEKICKS

Young men with hormones raging would do anything for this Jezebel though she was quickly aging.

I sensed the slut/her army against me but it wasn't conscious like today, I'd cry not knowing why.

The danger of hanging with sluts is not just immorality but the systems surrounding her like her army.

It was so horrible and powerful as an evil: her a haunted house and her men as minions of the devil.

This slut was the most dangerous woman I ever knew but that's in retrospect: at the time I was blind to it.

Narc abuse agenda: find someone in your circle who doesn't like you so they can collude against you.

They'll gossip, slander, rub your face in the dirt, make you feel like crap. All through history, that's their map.

The game is to make you feel inferior with them superior. They worm into groups used as their warriors.

She'd do anything to get under my skin. Invite me places outa home so she could attack with her gnomes.

SYSTEM DEVICES TO HURT YOU

These system devices have happened to you but perhaps just like me you were in blind denial too.

CHEAP SHOTS

Any slut is surrounded by an army of demons. Like attracts like: it's groups for your destruction.

She'd get bored/restless and cause trouble. When all else failed she'd let my dog out to watch me crumble.

I've never met a more destructive woman and it's all due to the many DEMONS in a slut, by definition.

The demons in her, her Johns, and all the demons in their doings. A haunted house of Satan, frightening.

I knew another man who was a whoremonger his whole life. He was insane, dumbed, filled with strife.

In this insane generation it's a feather in your cap to be a slut, a whoremonger, a lesbian or divorced.

I also knew many older women who shoulda been moral exemplars but instead were filthy unpaid whores.

Older women are to be exemplars of goodness but instead copy Blanche the slut in the Golden Girls.

The phony man says "don't say slut--that's not nice". But if the shoe fits, why not? The bible says it worse.

Many kids have to endure mom's boyfriends beyond locked bedroom doors. This is a HORROR.

If you've been abused by a narcissist you know what I'm saying. It's like what the hell? Things are insane!

It's so cheap and cheesy you can't quite believe it and don't wanna degrade yourself to think about it.

It's such a cheap shot that they'd post that photo or invite me somewhere to attack with her army of bears.

GET YOU OUTA THE HOUSE

CHEAP SHOTS

She seemed to wanna get me outa my house--my protection. Get me out for a group knockout.

I can't believe I went thru this but when young you don't realize the need for protection in your home.

The social narrative is "get outa the house, get out more". But that's false, you need a gate/locked door.

The social gnomes go crazy with coronavirus lockdown. But I've been in bliss for decades all alone.

Suddenly the Jezebel would rub stuff in my face--outa the blue triggering self-doubt, guilt and shame.

A good Christian lady friend who want's my best and isn't jealous--does such a woman even exist?

When she says "that looks great, please wear it more" she means "that looks terrible, please wear it more."

If a man goes to a whore he takes on ALL her spirits--tens of thousands of demons: just think of it!

ABUSE BY PROXY

Narcissists love to abuse by proxy--if you've learned nothing else here, that's the sick system Missy.

If they want to inferiorize you in some way or HURT you they will use other people. That's the system: evil.

Little teeny tiny digs are small stuff that adds up over time. Each pinprick accumulates 'til you're done.

They will either invite you out to put you down or not invite you so you feel ostracized from the group.

Her army doesn't have insight to what's happening--they will fight her victims without question.

CHEAP SHOTS

The narc/psychopath are notorious for wanting you to be around others who are your abusers.

The narcissist will encourage you to hangout with past abusers. "He wasn't so bad--be a forgiver".

If one recommends you go back to abusers they have very poor character and no empathy, believe me.

EX this mis-advisor out of your life. They are abusing you by proxy just by recommending that mean guy.

Once self-validating with healthy relationships you don't need to put up with crap to "feel connected".

In this social age you have entire groups who are nothing but flying monkeys for the main narcissist.

THE WEAK FIGHT THRU FLYING MONKEYS

Tho' less savvy than the narcissist, the flying monkey's goal is to hurt people doing her bidding, a sadist.

The woman is a sadist calling herself "good". Despite memes to self-justify she's nothing but a hood.

"Just sharing a beer" but she's about to abuse by proxy cuz she doesn't like getting her hands dirty.

Women love having an army of men used as sheriffs, sidekicks, punishers or even terminators.

Her minions are dumb--they don't have a clue as to what's happening but love the bedlam.

FLYING MONKEYS ARE DUMB ENFORCERS

If they can get gophers to do things FOR them they'll have em all lined up: the narc snakepit ready to romp.

CHEAP SHOTS

Watch out for anyone who's always trying to get you to go places. Leave your home to be disgraced!

The narc loves to hurt other people. They get a kick out of it--you heal by seeing this tho' it's unbelievable.

Depressed, sad, having bad things happen or feeling left out: the narcissist loves this tho' she's your sis.

They can't see women as abusers since they're weaker, not adding in flying monkeys, their enforcers.

When she uses her own son as a flying monkey things get cruel--cuz it's mom there's no stopping a fool.

The Baptist lady justifying the J.D.s became like the mother of a criminal gang, her only friends.

Women can be cruel keeping their own hands clean then dismissing thoughts of this terrible scene.

Since hurting you brings them joy they accumulate dumb gophers around em to enforce without question.

THIS IS WHY they travel in entourages, so they can use them as abusers and inflictors of damage/losers.

I knew one narc who'd come to my house with a group. I felt attacked just by that, nincompoops.

UNINVITED GROUPS ARE AN ATTACK!

To God's Few: When they come with an uninvited group they're bringing an invading army against you!

Unless you can vet every single person who comes to your house it's TOTAL disrespect, an ATTACK.

But did I know this, in those days? Tho' I was aggravated I couldn't put my finger on it and had to pay.

CHEAP SHOTS

TO THIS DAY I have PTSD from all I went thru the victim of flying monkeys goaded by her hanky panky.

I became aware of the evils of open borders by being invaded in my own home before I knew better.

You have serial bullies in families--opinion leaders--who have the whole tribe hating you as flying monkeys.

Sister ruled the mental mazeways for decades--everyone thinking the same/dissidents shunned as bane.

Husband, mother, sister: all tortured and banished cuz they couldn't be made to adapt to that crap.

And yet that was all due to denseness in her, blanket acceptance of the narrative of gross liberals.

What came first, the chicken or egg: Sister rejection or device used to adapt to the wretched one?

You have youth who are naturally conservative and the others dam liberals--imagine this boys/girls.

SERIAL SISTER BETRAYALS

She hurt me so much by her serial betrayals, backbiting and calumnies but that was dear sister Jane.

She killed my rep with everyone she met. Even strangers were told I was as bad as humans can get.

And then I'd be stuck in an archetype she created--a social hypnotic trance where I was the HATED.

In terror my devices used to adapt to this plight were the reason for the plight--making me weak not a knight.

You gotta get strong--repent of debilitating crutches--before you can bring down this evil bastion.

CHEAP SHOTS

When she couldn't convince me to give her what she wanted she got him to cajole me into it.

I said "I've already had this conversation with her, did she get you to come here?". Yes, always--it's clear.

She's too WEAK to stand on her own so she's developed a knack of collecting an army against your throne.

Flying monkeys in churches coming around to bother me to go to boring meetings. In coffee klatches.

After enduring this I became a total social recluse. I knew I didn't like it but never explained it all like this.

Flying monkeys are dumb and rev each other up. If you're their victim and they love hurtin', watch out.

"California Blackout": the sign reads on my wall. God has erased this whole era but I sure learned a lot.

CALUMNY IS HIX POLITIX

They do opposition research, try to figure out what makes Christians reject someone, then ruin him.

Poets are the unacknowledged legislators of the world. Percy Shelly 1821

They don't get her, she's different. They talk to her sisters who hate her and suddenly they're all in.

I never see anyone cuz they're all in their households. Quiet, order, predictability, security, folksy.

I've never been so creative since coming to middle America in a country neighborhood. Daily I start before midnight.

They say "we don't want revolution" so they can plausibly deny before they trigger it.

CHEAP SHOTS

As I learned in the desert, without a fence or a wall you're a sitting duck. However you can, wall up.

Youtube stars: What I learned from watching you is that popularity is no sign of truth.

Makes us sick: The bad architecture and art from hell goes along with dumbed down repetitive pop music.

ONE-IST thinking has degenerated our culture as the contagion of madness spreads like wildfire.

We could never criticize Obama for his policies because he was black. Imagine that.

Border control to stop a pandemic is now racist according to the WHO. That's how political correctness kills.

Bioweapons research has always gone hand in hand with depopulation agendas and we know the culprits.

Why are they doing it? They hate humanity. They also want abortion, dangerous vaccines, infanticide.

GLOBALISTS/DEMOCRATS PUSH DESTRUCTION

These same globalists push destruction of the family and demonize MALES: it's an anti-human agenda.

This virus has broken containment. It's out of control in China and they're covering up 1/4 million infected.

Evil is like a consuming fire that ignites everything it meets. The only remedy is ABSOLUTES which libs hate.

This generation is totally lost: stupid and debauched. The only remedy is Jesus/the certainty of the cross.

The cross settles it all. We are saved by faith plus nothing. A church demanding works is the FALSE church.

CHEAP SHOTS

Criminal illegal entry into America is now called "white supremacist" under the new way forward act.

The democratic party is the party of death, disease, demonic influences, destruction, destitution.

PREDESTINATION/PLAN OF SALVATION

You were saved NOT cuz you believed but cuz God chose YOU before the foundation of the world.

When you repented and became holy/blameless that's justification or INPUTED righteousness.

But it was by His love he PREDESTINED us to be adopted as His sons so all praise and Glory would go to Him.

So the whole plan of salvation was the outworking of His divine purpose: He chose US!

Before the foundation of world God determined WHO would be saved, written in the Lamb's Book of Life.

Come YOU the blessed of my Father to the kingdom prepared for YOU before the foundation.

Paul understood this: That we did not choose HIM but He had chosen US-- doctrine of election/predestination.

The doctrine of election/predestination is resisted by those who believe it's all OUR choice and "free will".

Those from a democracy [first great experiment] of total free will can't accept God's sovereignty ya know.

Those who have lived under monarchies of theocracies can accept better God's total sovereignty.

When you come into the Kingdom of God the Sovereign determines EVERYTHING and they hate this!

CHEAP SHOTS

It is by His will that we are redeemed, given forgiveness for trespasses and a beautiful future lavished on us.

Our inheritance is what He predestined on us according to His divine will and purpose--they can't stand this.

God predetermined this before, He KNEW us before. Then He predestined us to conform to His son's image.

Whom He knew He called, justified for salvation then GLORIFIED. This the "free-willers" despise.

You need to be born again from above--and you're not in charge when that happens.

A man can receive nothing unless it's been given to him from heaven, yet godless men crucified Him.

PATIENCE IS STRENGTH, SLOW TO ANGER

We are to be SLOW to anger. If in the spirit, patience is restraint that does not retaliate/anger is far away.

We should be those who are MARKED by loving kindness and grace, and EAGER to forgiveness.

You're not hostile or bitter from offense, your anger is far away--you are all-gracious and lovingness.

It's that high level of noble virtue that seeks only to do good. It is very rare--for where is KINDNESS?

In the end ALL relationships are destroyed from lack of forgiveness. Lost is the virtue of KINDNESS.

We were saved so that God could LAVISH us from the riches of His grace with deeds of kindness.

KINDNESS AND GOODNESS

CHEAP SHOTS

Kindness is the goodness of heart that intends the very BEST for others just as God does for us.

Kindness and gentleness is sometimes called "tenderness" for which Jesus is the model--we are to exhibit it.

And thus if kindness doesn't mark your life you're not a believer called to exhibit that quality of Jesus.

So kindness is a deep down virtue of moral excellence that very rarely does the world now experience.

This goodness is connected to righteousness--that's the stern, and it's soft side is goodness/kindness.

The king is to be like Jesus, that is righteous in judgement, tempered by goodness and kindness.

Goodness comes along with righteousness and softens it's convictions. It is NOT hard-edged, amen.

Do good to everyone but especially fellow believers. We're to be known for largeheartedness, tenderness.

FORGIVENESS

If you had 50 grand and had $50 stolen would you throw the rest away? That's unforgiveness, ok?

It's the little guy you gotta worry about. He's dumbed so insist you be social or it means you don't love God.

Lesbianism brings more violence than men. This is due to SIN which brings wrath, not "steroid drugs".

The individual [e.g. alcoholic] is to blame, not the rat-pack on TV that made drinking look classy/tame.

But people don't wanna blame the individual sinner, they wanna justify it or cast blame on all of America.

Just to placate their family/friends [get em off their back] they do worthless accomplishments--none of that!

I studied for 40 years and then I wrote 110 books in ten years after that--that's a fifty year **MATURE** work.

You do **WORTHLESS ACCOMPLISHMENTS** one after another just to please your friends. Be patient.

Around the studious productive introvert his friends say "when will it be done? I don't believe you."

They'd write me letters after years of dormant work saying "WE don't even believe you got a Ph.D."

You can't let your circle push you to produce. It's **NONE** of their dam business cuz God is the highest.

When God tells me to do something He also supplies the energy and endurance. Like 3-5 sleepless days.

TONGUES DO NOT EDIFY

The counterfeit of Satan is **NOT** the "work of the holy spirit" tho' they think it cuz it's so "ecstatic".

False religion in churches is very sensual, feeling-oriented, emotional, "mystical" with gimmicks and skits.

False religion stimulates the feelings and **EMOTIONS** not the thinking of the mind as scriptures indicate.

SENSUAL: Apprehended by the **SENSES** rather than the mind. The Good News brings joy not being blind.

The pagan ecstasies of speech that Paul described in page after page was **NOT** Christianity, ok?

PHONY revelations, tongues and visions dominated this early scene that Paul spoke of constantly.

CHEAP SHOTS

It's easy to fall prey to phonies so we must test the spirits: Jesus or Satan's energizing of disobedients?

Satan wants church to advance phonies: that's his business thru plastic surgery/drumming up ecstasy.

What should be going on is the speaking the word of God, not the chaos and confusion of tongues.

They got wrapped up in speaking pagan mysteries not edifying the congregation thru logical reasoning.

GIFTS ARE FOR EDIFYING MEN

All spiritual gifts are given for the purpose of ministering or speaking to men-- the opposite to pagans.

God was never intended to be addressed in a speech which is incomprehensible to the speaker.

You have missed the whole point. You're not speaking to God in a true gift but demons, not saints. Paul

He that prophesies speaks to men but tongues speak to no one since NO one knows what you're saying.

The true word of God comforts men, consoles them and gives em a fresh start again. Tongues: nothing.

The point of all gifts is to edify the church. Not edify yourself through flashy talents coming first.

If a brother takes a spiritual gift to edify the BODY and turns it to edify himself, he's wrecked.

DON'T CALL ME "FRIEND"

Don't call me "friend". I'll tell you when I want to, you don't choose me I choose you.

CHEAP SHOTS

Einstein's friends kept asking "When, WHEN will it be done?" and he replied: WHEN IT IS DONE.

Watch who you interview with. If they're a narcissist or jealous they'll sabotage you then publish it.

If someone ghosts you, you must cut em loose for good. Ghosting is selfish and rude, internet hoods.

Don't sit there in a quandary as to why they disappeared. In this selfish generation It's as common as dirt.

I heard my husband's caveat to not do the interview cuz "narcissists like that guy will SABOTAGE you".

SURE he wants an interview--so he can embarrass or make you look silly/inferior: be choosy or be blue.

A video interview is uncontrollable and permanent. I hate it and will wait for destiny and what God saith.

Rawfood rules: end day with starch [CHOKE]. European: start with pastry then go light to clear it all out.

Millions die each year from CHOKING in sleep. It's from FOOD so cure it easily: past morning don't eat.

If someone's gonna flake out, you don't need that cuz the whole world's become like that--unreliable rats.

Where they won't give credit where it's due, they are JEALOUS of you. See the signs or be blue.

Why should you talk to a man in an interview? He's a haunted house in interactions filled with poop.

CHOOSE YOUR OWN INTERVIEWER

Choose who your interviewer will be. I would like a gentle woman, with the questions so I can fully explain.

CHEAP SHOTS

I don't need to be interviewed by a competitive narcissist envious of me--that's a no-brainer, I've had it with thee.

If he has such poor character to flake out/disappear/ghost you my dear, of course that's it for the seer.

The narcissist's confidence is compensatory for low self-worth so he's not a big magnanimous guy, girl.

The glittering narcissist can't escape his low self-worth so will always suffer with your success dear girl.

Most complain as they get older no one cares. TRUE but God cares MORE cuz you are more just His.

Always remember consistency is character. If he's hot and cold and likely to ghost you again, why bother.

It's a matter of building healthy relationships--and knowing he can either step UP or step OUT.

In globalist Babylon, every human is just another brick. In God's eyes, each is important in himself: slick.

You must DESPISE anti-whitism and DEMAND people like AOC not be allowed to white-erase our people.

People like AOC actually see themselves as moral as viewed thru the anti-white narrative.

WHITE ANTI-WHITES ARE THE WORST

If whites don't speak up in response to blatant lies that we're "racist", like South Africa we'll ALL die.

Better to watch one good video 100 times as it changes your life than 1000 silly ones don't you think?

The most important thing about having pets: don't let those kids impose on em.

CHEAP SHOTS

They started to white-erase me at fifteen. I was supposed to be guilty for something tho' it didn't involve me.

There's something in the white DNA that's a tad complacent with invasion-- UNTIL THEY'RE NOT.

Never knew cats ate starch but when it comes to Panettone [Italian Fruit Bread] they eat all of it.

Breakfast: panettone/pizza. Afternoon: grapes/olives.

The modern church and the Mormons act as though being social is the key to salvation: false doctrine.

If you make an appearance, if you go to church/are seen, then you're showing your love for God. FALSE.

I wanted to stay home to and do God's MEANINGFUL work, they wanted me to GO here and there, bored.

How can Ms. Social Charm move up in church hierarchy and become an elder? She's a status climber.

Just like all of society the modern church has it's IN-OUT groups, desirables/deplorables, just like high school.

The modern church is SOCIAL and if you don't fit you feel unsalvageable. Free of all that, I feel lovable.

In the last forty years FAKE-LOVING is taking as GODLY and nothing could be more deceitful and nasty.

And the guy saying to BE NICE isn't nice at all. That's just his low self-worth clinging on to the social.

WHEN I HEAR TRUE PREACHING

When I hear God's true preaching on sin/repentance and heaven/hell I wanna be there, but it's rare.

CHEAP SHOTS

They don't talk about sin/repentance, heaven/hell anymore cuz it's all good, be nice, love yourself no matter.

What's valued is NOT God-fearingness but conformity to the group: that's the false church not the truth.

There's only one time you keep a man waiting: when you wanna say F-you. The Irishman

Usually three people can keep a secret only when two of them are dead. The Irishman

YouTube star uses Social Media as his pickup vehicle and constantly comparing and discarding people.

I now see him as a HAUNTED HOUSE--no kidding--and very silly and simple, no big thing really at all.

He has low self-worth covered over by glittering image which has become a BORE.

It's great to take a day to muse about progress of the last decade and its phenomenal God said.

I have youtube mentors whether they like it or not. It happens quickly by identifying then ridding rot.

Ontology is our world-view. If it's ALL ONE/it's all good BS then it IS you-- through and through: POOH.

I had the ontologically fatal insight in 1990 that we WEREN'T all one--it's a dam insult hon'.

The Christian DIVIDES, he does not UNITE. Unity is Satan, division is cuz you're a gentleman/good woman.

SOCIAL OR HEDGE OF PROTECTION?

In my first marriage I lost my hedge of protection as my husband insisted on being social/letting em all in.

CHEAP SHOTS

I wasn't allowed to vet anyone and had to adapt to em all. I was too young to understand the need for a wall.

You're **NOT** gonna get in here and make me adapt to you! You all seem grabby and officious as hell.

I just wanted solitude in my own oasis of otherworldliness but that was anti-social to him, a wino ass.

The narcissist is **ENTIRELY** in need of outer validation of importance/specialness & what an embarrassment.

I wasn't allowed to live **SOLO** in Borrego. Like any prison I had to chum up just for protection with amigos.

My present husband is a total fence for me, retired military. No one even tries to get into me, I'm **FREE!**

What feminists see as entrapment, the truth sees as **FREEDOM** for a woman: she's rid of vermin!

I was imposed on whenever I was single. It was **HELL.** The marriage is The Wall so she can now walk tall.

Messy people are shit and we can't stand to be around them. The most intelligent are **NEAT AS A PIN.**

FLOTUS did the world of women good when she said "If they don't love ME, to me they're dead".

What of adults using F talk? This is a sign of a louse and approval-getting from the younger crowd.

I'M NOT ALL ONE WITH THAT!

You say we're "ALL ONE"--with THAT? What a bloody gross insult, man--they are lower than rats.

You mean someone who lives like THAT--lifestyle--is equal to someone who lives like THIS, goodness/style?

CHEAP SHOTS

Sober, he was my loving fence. Drunk, he was all about social. I completely lost my [protection] hedge.

Drunk, he was Jolly Jimmy who was so mean to his wife in private. This social thing is a blight, shun it.

If this is entrapment or a cage, give it to me Sarge. It's either being imposed on constantly vs. enlarged.

Jezebel triangulates constantly. She's always raging about you to her friends who seem so prickly.

The MOMENT I got married the chaos/impositions stopped. It was a sudden clearing: me and God.

Suddenly, no one was bothering me! A lifetime of feeling like a cat in a roomful of rocking-chairs: FREE.

I don't have to deal with you and your personality anymore: your borrowing, disorder, triangulating or ghosting.

The spouse is someone you've agreed with. The others are untrainable--must have aristocratic reserve.

Panettone or pizza [homemade no soy], just V-8 later. I'm thinner than ever and feel so satisfied as a winner.

Just listen to music and you'll be amazed at what comes up. Outer entertainment/news is sad runner up.

She didn't want to press the issue since she was in sin too. That's how it works in contagious madness/poop.

PEACE AT ANY PRICE AIN'T EASIER

It seems easier to her to keep the peace any way she can then to demand repentance [or leave my home!].

If you've drawn a boundary--don't come here--and then renege on it--let him in--you're a dead woman.

CHEAP SHOTS

We've got to see the importance of **ENVIRONMENT**. Be a human ethologist: mal-adaptation is the sickness.

It seems easier to keep peace at any price than to demand repentance or get the hell out you louse.

Love pets by knowing how dependent they are on you. Give em a pet tho' there's other things to do.

Don't trust if he insists you palliate your words to be more "nice" at the sacrifice of truth: men or mice.

The more I clear the more I take on eternal wisdom from another realm--it was nothing I learned.

It's as though you access the **GREAT MIND** that ever lived. You know Shakespeare tho' you never read him.

In order to avoid chaos the great discoverer simply said "I've had a stroke" and he was free at last

I don't know why I was chosen as the vessel for the Great Work except I died to self at the hands of jerks.

There's no need to compete since we're all in our own stream which is entirely unique but not a freak.

What I give my husband is not my presence but his freedom after ordering his world efficiently.

WOMEN ARE HOME CREATORS

I've created a home [environment] to maximize his spiritual and intellectual unfoldment and he **LOVES IT!**

It's a team--he never woulda thought of my ordering principals or our stock I got in the house.

He woulda been happy leaving things that way--but I took notice of every inch and revamped it all, ok?

CHEAP SHOTS

I take care of the housework and books. He does the finances, problems, going out in cars/errands.

To get their ears back, women must make gold on their desire to fight husbands--the cultural narrative.

To get my ears back he turned a hose on me then all ran smoothly, each sentence ending with "honey".

Wife is GOADED by feminist friends to fight her husband and DISCOUNT him and he wants rid of em!

Must realize: her friends have MORE power with her than spouse--backed up by culture/media, false!

So husband wants RID OF her friends, for good reason. Now they all label him a fascist pig, isolatin'.

What an education it was to know her. A self-proclaimed vain slut like Blanche in the Golden Girls.

And if they all get involved with the authorities, they ALL hate men too and will make SURE he's the loser.

We were just passing ships in the night, you and I. I suppose I learned something so it's all right.

He wants rid of her girlfriends--she runs to tell them! Then they join forces and involve more against him.

If one is so into computer/TV, he's gonna do what you ask him to do halfheartedly you see.

BYE BYE OR BE DEAD

Narcissist traits: lying, gaslighting, triangulating, lacking empathy, objectifying, being vile and abusive.

Your inner circle is trustworthy, not like the world trying to do you in/overcome you or whatever.

CHEAP SHOTS

Most are liars/snakes--get that thru your head, ok? It's the default setting so your own must be trustworthy.

If you take em back after a major fault it'll be like you're chained to a tiger as they kill you that's all.

Once someone does those things/crosses those lines you say BYE BYE or don't come runnin' to me, see?

If you need to go thru a phone, just dump em. Everyone's cheating, that's the default setting, forget em.

The wrong person wipes you out/ruins your life. Be wise, vet thoroughly, get therapy, seek peace not strife.

If you break up for 2 days then forgive/go back to him, his badness had no consequences--it shows weakness.

You're weak if you can't breakup for two months. You've gotta get distance-- when stuff happens, get tough.

Men are really weak in relationships. He takes her back no matter what she does, fearing certain loneliness.

Weak people make threats but never follow through. This brings disrespect and then more trouble too.

The pain of leaving em is worse than being treated like shit. You prefer that to being alone without the twit.

Cultural relativism is used to justify everything and that's how we're degrading, devoid of all empathy.

It means you have no integrity, self-respect or backbone and especially over yourself--NO self-control.

Is it Trauma Bonding keeping you together? The association with PAIN making you want him/her?

They're not reaching out to YOU, but to what you can do for them--and you'd better get this thru and thru.

CHEAP SHOTS

So these people may miss you--but only because of the ease with which you brought them benefits.

THEY DON'T MISS YOU LIKE A HUMAN

They don't miss you in a human way and they're not contacting you because they care about you.

If they come in for the needed validation once it's given they're gone or whatever--you don't matter.

Just cuz he hits you up and says the right words doesn't mean he cares one bit: this is the view preferred.

They're missing a benefit from you: some routine, plan, propensity, past-time, buffet spread, drama.

It has **NOTHING** to do with you, it's always them. That's the narcissistic generation all around.

Once you find out who they are you're crazy thinking they'll change. It's face the truth or derange.

He does the finances, the errands and solves problems. The rest of the time OK internet and relaxation.

If you have em in your life, life's gonna be different. If they don't change you'll have to, it's mean and boring.

Your expectations are why you suffer. You think they'll be better with your nurture then you're hurt further.

The problem is not the narcissist but you can't have boundaries with the narcissist, a relational must.

WITHOUT BOUNDARIES LIFE IS RUINED

Without boundaries one's life is ruined in a relationship but these are impossible with the narcissist.

CHEAP SHOTS

With all loony stuff there are two options: break up or draw a boundary. Keep that always in mind to be free.

When you draw a boundary with the narc he'll lie, refuse to change or break up with you.

You can't win cuz the boundary won't work and the shitty behavior will continue, cementing your misery.

The narc has no object presence--if you're not there he's not thinking of you. That's why he's disloyal.

He'll be gone and won't think of you again until he needs you. It's a matter of the narc's perception too.

The narc will never miss you--the real YOU--and will never change because you can't set a boundary.

We must debunk the notion of bias or the disparate impact [on minorities] keeps the prejudice myth up.

Cancel culture is the same as throwaway or discard culture. With internet it's magnified for sure.

There's more criminality with blacks. It isn't about racism just facts, yet bias "explains" disparate impact.

The whole culture is declining as we hold each other down through bad advice or gossip-called-"concern".

The sure mark of a narc is triangulation: making you jealous with a third party or gossippin'.

Narc wants you off balance so they use this device: when it happens refuse the chance, see it/reject it.

THEY WILL TRIANGULATE WITH ANYONE

They will triangulate with everyone/everything that they can, it's their most powerful weapon.

CHEAP SHOTS

The narc will shit-talk or smear you with the new supply and then you wonder why they make you cry.

Since triangulation is their method of control, if you get too braggadocio or confident they'll use it, it's gold.

Triangulation works hand in hand with trauma-bonding. See yourself as irreplaceable for it's very damaging.

His control is making you feel like a dime-a-dozen throw-away so see yourself as totally unique, ok?

They don't see us as people but as objects. This objectification will kill your soul so see this.

He could never appreciate you/your complexities anyway--he doesn't even see you as a person, ok?

He wants to use you as a bank, a sex toy, someone to lean on/talk to when bored, a restaurant, a pit stop.

Since we're all capable of giving these things, he easily moves on. I was floored back then, it was no fun.

See yourself as uniquely irreplaceable [your narcissist-shield]: keep this front/center [never yield].

Knowing the narc signs is the therapy here. It will arm you so when it happens you're quick to eject the liar.

APPROVAL-GETTING IS VERY BORING

Saying what you think you're supposed to say, or avoiding what not to say is BORING, BORING, BORING ok?

You gotta speak truth/spit it out no matter consequences or it isn't creativity and it's out to lunch.

He lost his confidence and shook before the audience. That was the end of him for good, just a dunce.

CHEAP SHOTS

One narc said "my friends said they don't see what I see in you" and I showed him the door: new view.

I don't want you to come again cuz I can't get any work done. I don't like you/not happy when you come.

The only one replaceable here is the narcissist, after upgrading to someone who treats you nice.

Sex, money, attention: when he switches to the new supply it's no better, just someone different hon'.

Refuse to compete with his new supply. You are so unique in so many aspects the thought should make you cry.

You learn to spot a narcissist by the mind games they love to play. They lack empathy/are manipulative, ok?

Lacking empathy they're free to do whatever they please. They read people though, a contradiction it seems.

The narcissist doesn't care what pisses you off but he **KNOWS** what pisses you off.

The narc desperately needs that information to know what games to play. Understand this man, or die.

Tho' he couldn't care less personally, he's soaking up every detail of your life just to use it against you honey.

The narc controls you by feeding off your emotions. He wants you upset, sad, he'll take your animals.

STIRRING YOUR EMOTIONS IS HIS SUPPLY

To stir your emotions--his supply--he'll trip you up and piss you off. Endless cycles of grief erupt.

Don't ever go to his boring, puerile, egotistical page again. From now on YOU'RE the queen my friend.

CHEAP SHOTS

His severe superiority complex compels him to one-up you whenever he can: he's better than you man.

When lovebombing he was interested in you [got all your info] then he SUDDENLY devalues you with it bro'.

It's all because of what YOU did/do that makes it ok for him to do what HE did/does--that's the narcissist.

The narcissist either wants ALWAYS to be the hero or the victim and never the bad guy I reckon.

Just your suspicions should be enough. You don't need to go further--you just feel insecure and it's tough.

The right person will make you feel better. Not blame you, not shame you or make you worry ever.

This will heal your heart: Realize the narcissist doesn't want love, he wants admiration/approval.

The first stage of detachment is realizing it's not love with him, although he may have other feelings.

You begin relief when you stop taking blame for the person who is causing the issues. Out of reaction, whew!

As you recognize him you'll begin to care less and less about what he feels. This is great progress.

MOVE FORWARD, GO NO-CONTACT

When you start to move forward with your own life you'll finally go NO-CONTACT to avoid the low.

To end it for good, remind yourself how incredibly unhappy you are and how it's not working for you.

Make a list of what you want vs. what you have. They won't match up and you'll gain extra courage.

CHEAP SHOTS

In breaking free you must FACE how you allowed it all to happen for whatever reason. This is a hard one.

Finding what HOOKS you is getting to the ROOT of why you stayed so long. Did you make this happen?

God's great bounties and rewards aren't finite. My helping you get to your reward is great/no envy to incite.

You getting what you want doesn't mean I won't get mine. This competitive thing is very deceiving.

NARCISSISM IS EVERYWHERE

The narcissist has no ego/identity--it must be invented. They can adapt with great variety however wanted.

The narcissist can switch identities suddenly since there's no foundation for anything truly.

Thoughts, morals, hobbies and interests can change suddenly this way for there is no underpinning.

Most would be constrained from swift change by their own identity/ego but the narc is free to flip and go.

Their disordered self and inner problems don't change but their outer identity can change at any moment.

Everything on the surface is mutable: constantly in flux since there's no real identity there at all.

What are you gonna do, yell at someone in a rest home? All you can do is learn from the past and go on.

These hurtful lessons about people may sting in memory but just remember: no one knows your history.

CONTRIVED SURFACE PERSONALITIES

CHEAP SHOTS

He is contrived SURFACE personality, there is nothing underneath. That's the narcissist, an identity-thief.

Alone in the desert wilderness for 30 years, I built my inner foundation on baseline principals.

I did not build identity on status symbols or anything cultural but me, God, angels, elements, potentials.

I was happy with dogs and cats but when people came I was sullen as a desert rat--I learned from that.

I was evolving in solitude, they were not--as the cultural decline was like rot-- and I wanted them OUT!

They hurt me so much, these brief excursions with people, that I wrote 112 books about social evils.

Though brief they were enough to explode inside of me and fortunately I had a Ph.D. in Social Psychology.

I was held hostage in a sense to a gang of boys high school '85 in California-- the worst place on earth.

I was sheltered in a conservative home and to suddenly have this happen shocked and scared me.

These boys were terrible, debauched, lawless, violent, obtrusive, disorderly-- they thought they owned me.

Police wouldn't protect me [due to the ACLU] and my first husband was so drunk he didn't see a need to.

Once the boys saw the cops stood down, it was all downhill from there. That's the scene in liberal California.

Those boys are in their fifties now--should I yell at em about what they did as teens and can't recall?

FIRM FOUNDATION OF IDENTITY

CHEAP SHOTS

My firm foundation--after three decades alone--is solitude and my own creative essence coming thru **FREELY**.

People are so easily obstructed **SOCIALLY**. People think they own em, it's not wise to get involved honey.

I just wanna work but it took a lifetime to concretize the matrix so there was nothing obstructing that.

You went through the painful lesson cuz you still had to learn the lesson, period--you wouldn't listen.

Painful lesson: Don't get into a car and don't let anyone in your house cuz that's your protection from louse.

All you can do is laugh at it. It happened decades back, you were a sad sack, another person in fact.

You still hadn't learned the lesson so deserved everything you got. That's how it works now forget it.

Suddenly he saw he was nothing and sought only isolation. No more contrived identity to an audience man!

I didn't know about people in those days. I just let em all in, trying to be a good hostess.

Baptist lady they stayed with saw no fault, **EVER**--they all went to prison, she created criminals by waiver.

There's a force in everyone that is indestructible. Drill down, find it--you're a force of nature/able.

NARCISSIST IS TWO PEOPLE IN ONE

The narcissist is two people in one. Love bomb, then discard. Woo the clerk, hate your guts.

Once he flip-flops onto the devaluing stage, the discard is right around the corner--so disengage.

CHEAP SHOTS

Narcissist hates anything you love, refuses to give credit where it's due and rains on your parade: pooh.

Any success you have they'll scoff at or trivialize. It takes attention away from them: realize this.

Someone as selfish as the narcissist isn't going to like your success, not one bit--that's how you tell the twits.

Whoever does any of these things to you is TOXIC. Get out, block: stop labelling or even discussing it.

Lying losers, sluts or drug addicts are the default setting. Everyone's on probation with you the king/queen.

My imposers/invaders gave me lifelong gratitude now that every moment is mine/no interruptions of any kind.

As a fallen hero I realized with great shock how "friends" turned on a dime like I was street grime.

All archetypal psychiatry is the path of the hero. The fallen hero is KILLED by his associates and down he goes.

The immature trusts everyone but the mature trusts no man and the bible even says it. Recall Judas.

The higher your destiny the more you'll be betrayed, see? The devil in them hates the God you seek.

STOP GIVING UP YOUR PERSONALITY

Stop giving up your personality just to fit in/have friends. You'd do worlds better alone without offense.

Narcissism: no more diagnosis is needed. They suck, you're insecure, feel miserable and degraded.

It's a no-win situation. First he IDEALIZES you then when not "feeling" that emotion he devalues suddenly.

CHEAP SHOTS

You must be a narc-detective, a relational sleuth. Or your life can be ruined by who you date or do.

People are not mature anymore, they don't have marriage models to follow or mom may even be a whore.

Feelings and emotions VARY so as they vacillate the narcissist sees you differently and it's scary.

As their feelings change--as they always will--they will use some RANDOM reason to justify their change.

As their feelings change--as they always will--they will use some random reason to justify the discard.

These days the VICTIMS of people are seen as the bad guys when they dare to resist, accuse or discipline.

I was imposed on by those raised by social liberals who never taught the value of privacy/home ya' know.

Beware: the narcissist will re-idealize you when he runs out of supply whether for food/attention/sex/etc.

First they'll miss the SUPPLY then justify reconnecting then you're hooked and back in the ring.

REASONS ARE MEANINGLESS

Reasons are meaningless--it has to do with how you make them FEEL. If you draw boundaries, no deal.

The flying monkeys was how they hurt me the most: getting an army against me at a high cost.

Every narcissist I knew had the same pattern: his friends hated and rose up against me for no reason.

That's cuz the narc triangulates with everyone. He speaks against you to his friends just to relax--it's him.

CHEAP SHOTS

Especially if the narc is a Jezebel slut. Her low self-esteem compels triangulation against you with her friends.

Every time that toothless loser came here he brought an army. No gentleman does that honey.

They're narcissist losers doing this so of COURSE they're buttressed up with a monkey army--RESIST this.

The flying monkey army of the female is all her sisters and friends. You gotta deal with all of em.

One flying monkey is an associate reaching into your network to reject YOU in support of THEM.

Flying monkeys come from YOUR associates ruining your life or THEIR associates--systems are a blight!

When trapped/yoked in systems I felt like a cat in a roomful of rocking chairs and that'll never happen again.

Don't let people into your life or they can ruin it. Vet associates every one of em/their friends or forget it.

NOT JUST THE TOWN SLUT ANYMORE

It isn't just the town slut anymore, they're all like that. I didn't believe it at first but then thought about it...

Flying monkey armies: In extended families the narc will try to turn all her many relatives into his own allies.

It was a frightening shock to have all my relatives go on his side. I was double-betrayed by a monkey who lied.

In a social generation the narcissist wins thru charm and knows how to NETWORK against you, be warned.

Here I was gaslit by him but now everyone around me and him. My universe imploded, I was immature then.

CHEAP SHOTS

How was he able to turn my own circle against me? Cuz he's charming/charismatic and I had no clout.

He knew how to work me and knew how to work a room. I wasn't into that sort of thing, a social loon.

Despite his bravado the narc is insecure--compelling him to degrade or do everything for power/control.

Narcs have no tolerance for anything especially criticism. They take offense easily and I'd get rid of em.

Creatures of habit they hate changes to the status quo or being told "no". You're afraid of their reaction too.

NARCISSISTS HAVE A SHORT FUSE

Short Fuse. Narcs have a really bad temper and are impulsive in a fever: don't let him in, refuse.

Due to early abuse the narc trusts no one. These are black coals ready to flare up so he hates everyone.

It's hard to believe a braggart is self-loathing but that's the compensation. He hates himself and you too hon'.

The narc underestimates people so when the latter's had enough and discards him, he unravels.

He thought he had me figured out/set then I flipped the script by getting outside help and he was gone.

Because after a while the narc is no longer interesting just a dam drain and you hate seeing him coming.

Narcs are totally paranoid. This happens when your entire life is a lie which in time increases complexity.

Narcs fear abandonment due to lack of trust. Worse, they can't abide a boundary laid down, a relational must.

CHEAP SHOTS

A narc knows deep down you'll eventually leave but in the meantime will shit-test you/continue to deceive.

Narcs hate being alone. That's why I couldn't get rid of him and he dropped in all the time. God, come!

Today I'd say "I want to be alone--I don't want anyone around". But back then I let him in, dethroned.

We've a constitutional right to privacy, solitude, to be alone with ourselves. We should put it that way elves.

As family dysfunction grows so does narcissism everywhere. We gotta defend against liars.

They fear abandonment yet they ghost, they go dark, they ice you out or give silent treatment.

Fear of rejection is why they cheat or have a narc harem full of fresh meat. Don't get involved, sweet.

NARC HAREMS

A narc harem is just constant new supply he keeps on the bench, then it doesn't hurt as much if one rejects.

A narc harem is fresh meat for em to grab onto should you bail out. Listen up: they always gotta have that.

You will never be enough for them. Supply is like air to a narcissist--they need it constantly: write that down.

He hates rejection/indifference. We all hate it but being admired is his whole reason for living I guess.

Number one, know you can't change them. If you can't walk away then put up with scum/no fun.

If you're dealing with a narcissist accept them or don't-- you've only two choices with a stubborn goat.

CHEAP SHOTS

Set boundaries. Narcissists HATE boundaries and will do everything they can to see you have NONE.

The people who don't want you to have standards are those who can't meet your standards.

They hate boundaries cuz they want what they want when they want it and you're not gonna block it honey.

Test me: lay a boundary and you'll be ghosted, given the silent treatment or discarded. However, persevere.

If you set boundaries but don't follow through, don't bother cuz now the WORST will be coming to you.

If you don't back it up and do what you said you will do the narcissist sees you as a joke/more yoked.

Narcs want everything to be your fault even his cheating. Don't accept responsibility for ANYTHING.

Grey Rock is to just disengage--it's classic detachment. Become boring, no more fights engagement.

He needs to go somewhere else because THAT doesn't work here anymore. With time disengage more.

RAPID CYCLING

Every time you give in/start over the cycle will get faster. Idealize, devalue, discard--don't bother.

You know the B.S. he's gonna pull and he knows how you'll react to it. Careful here, it can get very dangerous.

Know these weaknesses to not get involved with something getting worse: "rapid cycling".

Anyone victimized by a narcissist must re-find themselves, their core identity--it takes time for a new reality.

CHEAP SHOTS

When the narc is injured [due to a boundary or reaction] you're gonna get a smear campaign, ok?

After the discard you may eventually be hoovered [drawn back] by a flying monkey doing his dirty work.

A flying monkey works in behalf of the narcissist who is the puppet master. This really shows the coward.

When sweet talk doesn't work you're gonna get something drastically worse, prepare for an outburst.

FEMALE NARCISSISTS

20% of narcissists are females. Their number one trait is fierce competitiveness even on trivial details.

The female narc depends on others for supply--to mirror back to them how beautiful they are all night.

With a new female in the group she must either delete her or make her cater by aligning with the others.

The female narc is alpha of her group--the new one must be an obedient source of supply or regroup.

Anyone who threatens the female narc in the group better get in line or she'll be removed quickly too.

As her daughter becomes an adult she ignites mom's fears of inferiority and it becomes a competitive blight.

The narc mom may have serious enmeshment issues with her son. When he takes a new wife, look out hon'.

The son's marriage triggers intense jealousy with mom whose active competition with wife begins.

NARC MOM JEALOUSIES

CHEAP SHOTS

The narc mom's attempts to retrieve the attention and love of her son will wreak havoc on the new union.

The female narc is overly concerned with appearance: hers and her family's. The image is perfect, see.

They're not interested in what truly matters but obsessed with appearances and it's superficial, all of it.

She's not interested in character and values--except in a phony sense when she uses that as an excuse.

If she's a churchgoer it's ALL about appearances and she has no interest in sound doctrine, she is spiritless.

Despite her image of confidence she's incredibly jealous and with her posse of friends will evil gossip.

She's oversensitive to criticism even when constructive: it's always a narcissistic injury and she hates it.

A normal conversation you can't have. She's not interested in any reality where she's not perfect love.

DRAMA QUEENSHIP

The female narc is a drama queen. She's bored quickly so what gets her going is an explosive scene.

She'll use big, bold histrionics when describing herself and make a production out of it. Stories by a twit.

The extreme dramatics about herself will always be a present feature of the female narcissist.

She's extremely good at triangulation, pitting people against each other--she's a soul killer.

Narc mothers are proficient at causing fights between siblings. A devastated life is explained by this.

CHEAP SHOTS

If you are unfortunate enough to have a narcissistic mother in law she will be a BIG problem all in all.

She will display her wares and dress provocatively to get her supply--with the years this is misapplied.

The narc female has affairs. She will usually choose new supply from her own partner's circle of spares.

She has no ethics/morals when it means getting what she wants, she'll get supply from wherever it comes.

The female narc has a shameless disrespect for boundaries. She's always welcome she thinks.

She thinks everyone else's belongings are available to her. It isn't stealing when she takes em or whatever.

She has no respect for your personal space. It's hers, your discomfort is tough, you should be pleased.

Try to lay a boundary, her behavior won't change and she'll continue to invade you night and day.

She uses rudders of control. Excellent at silent treatment or cutting you off from affection/sex ya know.

NARC EXPOSURE WEARS YOU DOWN

Exposure to the narcissist will wear down your own values and beliefs. It rubs off, you're jaded without relief.

Then a once kind and compassionate woman becomes a catty cruel materialist liar just like her husband.

Female narcs lack sympathy, feel entitled, are exploitative and take advantage--but it's covered up.

Coverts are more sneaky and passive-aggressive with their abuse tactics while overts are out with it.

CHEAP SHOTS

She's the victim--that's her reason for being. May seem needy but her victimhood draws freebies.

Top trait of the female narc: exaggerated and phony EMPATHY to get something in return you see.

Female narc loves to blame and shame cuz it puts her in the power position of giving out the ill fame.

Shaming and blaming feeds her ego cuz the name of the game with all narcissists is CONTROL.

The female narc has VERY loyal and vicious monkeys ready to do her dirty work. Get away, avoid and shirk!

She'll always send her flying monkeys out to viciously attack you just to get her wishes through.

YOUR OWN MOTHER SABOTAGED YOU

It's very hard to comprehend your own mother has been sabotaging you your entire life. Gossip: rife.

She portrays herself as the most loving and gracious mom in the world. See "Mommy Dearest" girls.

Narc mothers refuse boundaries. Establish one and she'll go ahead and snoop/impose without quandary.

The narc mother will divulge embarrassing/humiliating information about you to perfect strangers.

She's famous for stealing the spotlight from her daughter or others. Whomever she envies she'll smother.

Narc moms are unforgiving: If you've offended her slightly she'll NEVER forget and bring it up incessantly.

THE NARCISSIST IS EMPTY INSIDE

CHEAP SHOTS

The narcissist has **NOTHING** inside so is totally addicted to outer approval/admiration, it's so obvious.

He lights up with admiration and continues talking about nothing getting more laughs from the peanut gallery.

The problem with codependency is enmeshment with someone else--it becomes your whole sense.

It's when your feelings of worth and value don't come from the inside but persons or people on the outside.

You weren't taught to validate yourself so your whole life is **PEOPLE** to do it and it's a desperate **MUST**.

You drive anyone crazy with an inner life due to the masses you always have around you, it's a lie.

You don't know what you feel since you weren't taught to find your own feelings and inner environment.

She was so codependent she "swallowed" [INTROJECTED] her mother then proceeded to embarrass her.

When I separated from the fused system the strange behavior stopped and I was normal again.

The only enmeshment-protection is building your own value system--you **KNOW** what to believe man.

Whenever you feel objectified in **ANY** way especially your age, back off--it's a horrible plight and tough.

FORGIVING THE NARC MOM

Narcissists seek out the broken, the vulnerable, the creative, the passionate and more intelligent.

I wrote it all ending with the narc mom who sabotaged her at every turn--a turning point ending the curse.

CHEAP SHOTS

Before you can forgive the mother [a catalyst to new life] you must first see what she did--gossip/strife.

She undercut you constantly by degrading you to other people even strangers. Narcs are controllers!

That alone, along with taking you outa lessons where you had success, is what you have to forgive I guess.

It could be she SO pissed you off inwardly, perhaps repressed, that it ruined life/created a mess.

BARE ESSENTIALS ON THE POTTER'S WHEEL

Fallen hero syndrome brought me down to bare essentials in a cabin THEN I started to build up again.

If all tied up in external sources of selfhood you don't know where to begin: start with your VALUES son.

This cuts the need for approval for every single thing you do--like a little baby starved for attention too.

Within a day of being in my cabin in the desert wilderness I felt a TON drop from my soul--it was BLISS.

What woulda put most in an existential PANIC was my freedom to be with God free of lunatics.

In my tiny cabin I looked out the window and sensed SPACE, freedom, God and natures ELEMENTS.

I was so happy with just a cabin and a bike, I wanted to live there for the rest of my days high as a kite.

I was amazed to realize I didn't need all that stuff at all, what I needed was SOLITUDE, free of y'all.

This was an amazing insight about my self, also coming to God at the same time--I was free at LAST.

CHEAP SHOTS

Instantly I felt the crushing weight of all old systems slip off my shoulders, I saw how I had been bothered.

Paul found it when he went to prison. Sometimes God has to consign you down to just a desk and a pen.

I saw how both women and men gossip for control--how I feared their evil utterances for decades now.

I was SO glad to be free of human society and all their "rudders for control" like telling everyone all.

My mother and sisters gossiped about me constantly to anyone who'd listen--I was free of social vermin.

All human manipulations are rudders for control and they'll use em all. Solitude is the only freedom y'all.

WANTING ATTENTION IS AN EMBARRASSMENT

When I see you doing anything for attention/getting off on admiration it makes me think of my first husband.

The narcissist: without any inner validation all he does is for approval and attention--don't trust him.

If someone is empty he gets lonely/seeks to narcissistically work a crowd who applauds him.

When I see a narc I know it and in solitude I regained more strength, power and confidence every minute.

When enmeshed with other people you CONSTANTLY want their approval. Enmeshment is evil.

All of that is released when knowing you can make your own decisions from your own ethics/value system.

Once solitude and God was my base value system it built up geometrically from there until a seer.

CHEAP SHOTS

Since I'm non-social my values are beauty, housekeeping, tasty meals, pet care, music, love of home.

As a scholar I leave time uncommitted to study and write which is 80% of my time, there is little else.

So that's my value system: God, solitude, home, work and **NOTHING** will ever enmesh me again, my win.

In social generations "friends" are the whole thing--I feel sorry for em! Do they share your values man?

Cuz if they don't you'd be **FAR** better off alone. Trust God to fill your cup/for your daily bread and be gone.

In my 31 years in the desert wilderness I saw people as just an encumbrance--to a different beat I danced.

FRIENDSHIP OR VALUES?

To have a friend you may have to give up your values and that's too much to ask so I say **NO**.

These values were too hard-won--the first time I was able to talk to anyone was when I met my husband.

Everyone I met before were zombies, hypnotized to the current narrative, unempathetic, boring, cold.

If a friend does things outside of your value system then you're be judging them: it's **NOT** freedom.

I was alone in the desert and the "friends" I had were totally unlike me in every way--I hated it ok?

People are bored/lonely so they'd visit me and that was **HELLISH** cuz I had evolved/they were still stuck.

They held me back then. They were debauched and I didn't wanna hear about it--shut up man.

BUILD AN INNER IDENTITY: ELEMENTS

Bare essentials were the ELEMENTS: rain on a tin roof, breeze in the aft, stars at night, early rise.

And ALL ELSE was human superfluity and non-essentiality I wanted no part of, I wanted to stay home really.

These people don't know what's going on/couldn't care less if they did, it's a DROUGHT the bible said.

So now you're whole, BE that refreshing breeze but don't allow boundary busting ever again teach.

They're so social--to get their validation--they don't ever think how they ruined your privacy, it's a given.

Getting privacy and time alone is a fine art and a life's work. The world seeks to invade like a curse.

Only now, after a lifetime of feeling invaded, do I have that wonderful privacy on acreage with a locked gate.

This was my greatest achievement: first, seeing that I needed it and second arranging the new life.

He was "social" or too dumb to see we needed protection from [or at least the ability to vet] people.

IF THEY'RE SOCIAL THEY'LL LET EM ALL IN

If they're social they'll let em all in on you and for a deep empath it's the human zoo and horrible too.

After the WAR when you were victim you rose up again as they were taken away to death camps: inversion.

After the WAR you must appreciate every moment of relieved bliss not memories of that, or this.

CHEAP SHOTS

They interfered in your life but then after all, you allowed the interference and strife.

You just have to face it was a **DEMON**, beyond that there was no rhyme or reason so realize it and go on.

With codependency you're enmeshed: easily allowing abuse and past stuff shoved in your face.

The reason we're depressed sets off the chemical imbalance and anti-depressants do the rest.

One major reason for depression is **ANTI-DEPRESSANTS. And 70% of American women are on em!**

The **MAIN** problem is invalidation of the **CORE. I can FEEL** those feelings tho' I can't remember as a toddler.

He was higher when I was needy but when I went up he's nowhere to be found--it's all explained finally.

HOW TO ERASE THE WAR IN MIND

Don't think of em in their hay-day with you as victim. Think of em NOW: total losers after the system inverted.

Don't get specific in memory--just see it as **THE WAR** and don't think of the individual soldiers.

We all have bad times--soul-wrenching eras--cuz it's part of the hero's path from rocky climb to sublime.

I had to go through all that--it lasted decades. Being a total victim of losers and I had no defenses.

If in sin God will remove your hedge of protection then the evil world flows in like a tidal wave I reckon.

It's not about individual players but the **WAR** you went thru to overcome all you had to and to learn who's who.

CHEAP SHOTS

Now I live in protection and beauty but know how fast I can lose it so do everything to stay right with it.

Don't get into the bloody details in mind! It was **THE WAR**--put it all in a bag and then throw it all out.

I'm at my highest intellectually, spiritually, artistically, musically, emotionally so age is a good thing see.

Age is not dwindling. As the body recedes the temporal lobes burst open to reveal [panoramic] eternity.

Eternity is viewed panoramically and for an artist or writer it's thrilling when the temporal lobes open quickly.

Anything which widens your vision or expands your mind beyond your petty problems is relieving.

You were a loser's victim **THEN** but you're **NOT** now, the system has changed: your memory's deranged.

ETERNITY VIEWED PANORAMICALLY

The sick system with you one down was a function of how weak you were at the time not the great "him".

This was your **WAR** and you got through it. Compared to other war victims it was really nothing, know it.

Even some of your foes helped you along the way, but when things reversed they were taken away.

These toothless losers, stealers and dealers, fools and tramps: see em as characters--ARCHETYPES.

Part of the hero's journey is learning about people after being naive--how the lower archetypes deceive.

Stop thinking about Mary and Henry and start seeing everything as an archetype--this clears memory.

CHEAP SHOTS

It is a terrible thing to fall into the hands of an angry God and I did, He got me good and I was humbled.

You're a God-denier going after Eastern religions man. You are empty and foolish, your eyes are blank.

And now you're parents yourselves, acting that way. Each generation is worse from the hippies.

Being weak and boundariless demons got in and made you act like that. Let it be, forget it all as God has.

The demons of ego and social acceptance: these also gave you license but forget the embarrassment.

Now you're the king. The king isn't labored with feelings of victimhood from way before he knew anything.

HIX POLITIX STINKS

Erdogan is not just turning against Greece but Our People--the WEST--as a biological reality.

It's race desecration thru miscegenation and now mass immigration. It's the WEST he hates son.

Anti-Whiteism means ANTI-WEST: A desire to bring down everything we are though it was the best.

There would be no democratic party without racial division so they keep opening the wound. Tucker Carlson

The Party of Inclusion has become the opposite. That tent collapsed except for victims of identity politics.

AOC is the rising star of the godless left and she'll do and say anything to normalize sin or call it the best.

We all see Soros putting judges, mayors, police chiefs in--to maintain sanctuary cities and the criminals in em.

CHEAP SHOTS

Due to fake news liberals in California think Mafiosi Pelosi's a big hero for going after President Trump.

Soros plans to take over America thru his sanctuary cities so he packs em with mayors, sheriffs, judges, D.A.s.

Germany needs to develop a new approach dealing with aggressive men shaped by patriarchal cultures.

Western civilization is seat of liberty, freedom and extraordinary accomplishment but we won't hear that.

How fragile is a system where government is restrained by rules. All over the world tyranny is so cruel.

They're mean to everybody, not just you. It helps to see the universality of it now.

Dependence on mass immigration is a sign of societal weakness and a structural defect. Mark Steyn

From California chaos to order, decency, familial atmosphere, kids that obey, quiet homers.

What a difference an orderly society makes after being in that leftist atmosphere where kids rule us folks.

It's always OP-TRUTH: They DO wanna civil war but blame it on us. They're getting ready to false flag/trigger it.

If you invert what they say, nine times outa ten you'll get the right answer. Alex Jones

They agree to look reasonable for few months hoping you don't have a memory then they trigger false flags.

MOST CAVE IN TO ATTACK

Most people aren't like a Karen Kellock who gets more hardcore under attack--most just sell out.

CHEAP SHOTS

It's best not to know rather than to know and still do it. Jesse Lee Peterson

World Government Until: Welcome to where time stands still. No one leaves and no one will.

Suicide in America up 40% . Biggest sector is blue collar workers ruled by tyrannical indifferent elites.

Frauds of British radio: Totally down-putting demographic change when it's as plain as your face.

The FLAG symbolizes all of us--burning it is self-destructive and we cannot allow it.

My identity's unimportant--it's what I know, what I've accomplished, what my beliefs are. Heather MacDonald

Unbelievably, parents of college students care more about prestige institutions than the actual education.

"Disparate Impact from Bias" means: the reason one doesn't do as well as me is cuz I'm a dam racist, see?

RELATIONAL SCIENCE

It's become a fine science and you can get a Ph.D. in it: How to handle relationships on social media.

Avoid the phase of pleasing the world with silly phrases or words. Transcend, don't conform to the herd.

Inferiors will always have their monkey army while you do not, you're too deep and don't have time for that.

We have intuition for a reason: to beat the games of people like this when most of it lie hidden.

SYSTEM DEMANDS THE SOCIAL

Every system I was in fought me on it. I was to be social, not go into withering solitude--you're locked in.

CHEAP SHOTS

Students are being taught to hate: from the greatest works of civilization to each other, ok?

New age is ONEISM, the Truth is TWOISM. Good and bad, true and false, male and female, saved vs damned.

I look forward to the future with glee. Cuza what Christ did for me, repentance and you I'm finally free.

You thrill my soul, but this degree of sensitivity is only possible because of redemption and the gospel.

GENETIC UNDERTOW: WATCH IT NOW

If empty on the inside one will soak up his culture or environment--if it's sick he's a lunatic.

I had no idea why I acted that way. It was in the system, the genes, generational curses--when weak, ok?

When weak we "click" into these negative proclivities and all symptoms roll out. When strong, NOT.

When I clicked into these genetic proclivities I felt carried along in a storm surge, it was a tragedy.

When thru solitude, self-awareness, study and God I gained strength, these proclivities had no effect.

They were horrible, being dragged down to the lowest of the collective unconscious: a terrible dark realm.

Living good, decent, repentant and orderly keeps me on top just bobbin' along. No problems, a lovin' home.

With everyone knowing their duties and doing them, the home runs like a Swiss watch--you can expand.

WAIT FOR IT TO COME TRUE

CHEAP SHOTS

If creativity is self-generated--if you don't wait for it to come thru--it will be boring and empty too.

I'm done with my work and now just choose the music for the day. Constant ordering, sweeping anyway.

Stop raging over past imposers and just remember: they were doing God's work in punishing a sinner.

You got as you gave. You were a sinner and so you had nothing but problems with people esp. losers.

When you repented the dust settled and all went smoothly. No more energy vampires coming around begging.

I look back aghast at how dangerous it all was. I had no idea being in denial/addicted and life was tough.

The answer to all evils is to stick to your own work, love it and love fans of it. All/everyone else, forget it.

SLOGANS OF MEAN PATHOGENS?

Them saying Diversity Strengthens is whatcha call a "mean pathogen" cuz they conquer thru the division.

The world is filled with billions geometrically multiplying fast and we must have **BARRIERS** or be lost.

Socialism: philosophy of failure, creed of ignorance, gospel of envy and equal sharing of misery. Churchill

He had Intermittent Explosive Disorder [IED] so what could I do but ban him from coming to my door forever?

Spanish Flu pandemic in 1918 when millions died: how fast it spreads and what happens to the dead.

The churches have fallen and gone is true doctrine. They don't even call for repentance often.

CHEAP SHOTS

"How did you go bankrupt?" Two ways: gradually, then suddenly. Ernest Hemingway

God said I'm wasting my time trying to find something here to edify my mind. It's a FREE mind that's fine.

He brought hell in on me inadvertently. We walk in muddy waters, not everyone is safe thru autoimmunity.

MARRIAGE IS NOT OBSOLESCENCE

"He's holding me back" is no excuse for divorce. That's not what marriage is: liable to obsolescence.

The feminist seeks to "go on ahead" like he's holding her back and ends up bankrupt/alone: a sad sack.

An alcoholic can't take cough medicine/Nyquil without lighting that fire. It's genetic/easily triggered.

If you wanna be famous for whatever reason overexposure is your enemy--you should be a mystery honey.

I create content all day long but don't call myself a "content creator". Get offa your perch loser.

Let US decide if you create worthy content, not YOU deciding you're all that great/benevolent.

I'm a writer--my words are read after my death. It isn't necessary to see what I look like God said.

You're great at marketing yourself--hallelujah. But what about just the subject at hand and forget ya.

Better watch out, content creator: as fast as they brought you up they can tear you down/it's embarrassin'.

SLOW AND STEADY: FOUNDATION

CHEAP SHOTS

Slow and steady, that's the way. Not self-aggrandizement and selling yourself with no foundation, ok?

Oh well, it's basically a moral issue and you may have to go off on a tangent to learn that, hope not.

I feel much freer away from all that ego stuff. I'm into hard work and knowing the subject matter not fluff.

It's basically sickening, disgusting and ego-gratifying with long weird pauses without a valid reason.

An over-elucidation of non-issues that don't really matter just to fill content cuz you set a precedent.

I just wanna write when I wanna write and NOT when I don't, not adapt to a schedule wiping you out.

Either it comes thru or it doesn't. You seem forced many times--this is not creativity and it's boring.

You're the spout, God's the flow. Not you so brilliant acting like you're in the know making it up as you go.

SHAME is the result of narcissistic families. Caring too much what they think is the SYMPTOM see.

I just went my way/matured and she stayed the same and BANG it was a war and I can still feel it dear.

Family dynamics, machinations and interrelations can create such evil havoc before we're free of it.

ENMESHMENT IS THE PROBLEM

What I went thru when enmeshed in family dynamics was so horrific on a calumnious soul murder level.

Enmeshment means you've got their demons in ya and depending how intense you are, good luck to ya.

CHEAP SHOTS

They're dead, near-dead or the walking dead but you've got a great and prosperous future instead.

Liberals run life like nazi Germany and they WILL come against thee, ganging up on dissidents, see?

God's man is an individual--Americana--but liberals hang in groups, herds and klatches to talk about ya.

My life in the new age boomer herd was sorrowful and sad. Things always went awry and they justified bad.

I know what it's like to go bad and completely be thrown out of grace. A disgrace, your identity defaced.

It was a case of mistaken identity and they'll know it now. It's God pouring hot coals on their head, wow!

It was a horrible system and I don't know if it was me, the demons in them or just discrepant information.

I find cruise ships claustrophobically crowded and would never dream of consigning myself to one.

I saw one hour cruise advertisement and to me it was a HORROR show--all those crowds ya' know.

SOCIAL CONTAGION: FLYING MONKEYS

When around em I felt I was in an evil den. Unhappy, depressed and pessimistic from triangulation.

I felt like wrenching, surrounded by demons! This was how I felt ever since kindergarten until my isolation.

Suddenly all their friends are against you too: those are their flying monkeys making you miserable.

Humans will turn against you for no apparent reason. Cuz they talked to someone--it's a social contagion.

CHEAP SHOTS

The sense of such soul treachery surrounded by ignorance, secret alliances and quarrels.

She imposed on me and I imposed on her right back. Even tho' I didn't have a right to, it's a fact.

It's all wiped out now, like a piece of cake down the sink. It was all just a bootcamp for you and a mystery.

SOME CRAZY WOMEN ARE TRAITORS

Some crazy women are traitors to America and our president. Don't get close again--they are DEMONS.

How could some crazy women be so ungrateful to our president when he's been so good to us?

Don't worry, they'll eat their words soon. That's always how it happens when God uses the "buffoon".

He propounds non-issues then goes out on a limb to defend them, bringing his whole house down.

I won't ever go there again cuz it's an insult to my intelligence and he just wants to get back.

Doggedly he sticks to his old premises tho' long ago we were bored with it. Here we go again you twits.

Anyone who goes to those extremes to propound their false ideas are eventually cut down to size.

DEMORALIZE YOUTH IS THEIR AIM

How non/anti-LBGTQ of me to say that.

Demoralize the youth is their aim. You can't have liberty but you can have endless sex, that's their game.

Globalism is disdain for religion and morality. It pushes perversion to control us starting in kindergarten.

CHEAP SHOTS

You can't defend yourself with guns nor have free speech but you can have plenty of kinky sex--this stinks.

With those youth hormones raging it's all they think about but sin brings wrath--they're angry a lot.

So the globalists have them hooked and **DOWN** thru condoning sex sin and luring em in again.

Hollywood, hip hop, gangsters, red carpets, fame culture are all part of the plan, don't you see man?

Virus fears will make us stay home more and that's good. We run around too much getting nothing for it.

NARCISSISTS HAVE CLOSED MINDS

A narcissist is so other-directed he can't possibly have a wide, absorbent, supple mind. It's all **HIM**: boring.

Face it: You inwardly disagreed with everything he said. You saw him as dangerous as many were misled.

Their reality is built on nothing but tired traditions and blood relations. They never dug deep man.

They know nothing, just sponges to the current narrative. Tho' fake news is folding it's still in their relatives.

Tho' he put the whole country in danger he dressed cool and hung out with billionaire hip hoppers.

LET HIM REMOVE THE STAIN/GIVE SECURITY

His responsibility is atonement and security, ours is <u>faith and hope.</u>

They had experienced God's perfection but now they didn't believe Him—right there in His presence.

CHEAP SHOTS

Because they didn't believe God they were catapulted into sin and depravity as He gave them up suddenly.

Despite beautiful surroundings and opulence--everything at hand--human dramas ruin everything, amen.

Warning: violence is the default setting even with women. Pugnacity prevails, not like when we were children.

Troublemakers are no more--you look for them and they're gone forever like they weren't there before.

You can have the combo of early trauma and strong astro sign and end up with a lunatic but later a real find.

If you do evil God will have no reason to mention you cuz you get named by doing the will of God.

CHEAP SHOTS: ALCOHOL AND ANOSOGNOSIA

Alcohol is like lighting a fire. Is it worth it to START if you can't STOP?

I hated that crap. You may not get drunk/make a fool of yourself this time but Satan waits/has patience.

So he takes a little Jagermeister at night: a German licorice anti-coronaviral elixir, that's alright.

What's the use of starting if you can't stop, are compelled to drink more and thrown into sins galore?

I had the inability to stop once having started. An immediate loss of control, chemically blocked.

It's called Anosognosia--the loss of pattern recognition. That's the end of learning then spiraling down.

The mere atom of alcohol brings anosognosia and now you're no longer the captain of your ship.

CHEAP SHOTS

Satan sits on my shoulder urging me to drink so he can take over. It's an ever-present danger.

With anosognosia you're killing yourself with the simultaneous inability to see you're killing yourself.

To be an evolving human you must see your patterns and correct them. With alcohol this is impossible man.

NO SOCIAL DRINKING FOR ALCOHOLICS

There are so-called intellectuals who push "social" drinking for alcoholics. They try it and die as lunatics.

When I drank alcohol what felt like "relief" was actually someone else taking control like a thief.

If I took one drink or swig of Nyquil there was no telling where I'd end up--into Satan I was swept up.

Prisons are filled with those who did horrific things while drunk and they can't even remember it.

Ray doesn't have my genetic predispositions so he can have a little jagermeister before bed he said.

My relatives in Scotland were either great and famous orators and evangelists or gutter alcoholics.

There is no middle ground with greatness. You either do your thing or will be mowed down like the grass.

As genetic alcoholics our inability to STOP once having STARTED is biochemical inevitability: <u>it's not US.</u>

Life is a million times happier without alcohol. I'd never wanna wake up like that again, it was HELL.

I know what happens to animals from pure absentmindedness so stay clear/be nice.

CHEAP SHOTS

FOOD/ALCOHOL COMPULSIONS

Food means mother and is a problem with broken bonds. Once I lost control and ate a whole bag of Cheetos.

When I filled out my inner reality food was no problem at all. In fact it's a chore to fuel up at the pump.

It was an inner bottomless pit I could never fill. It was an emotional illness leaking into biology girl.

I could never fill this inner cavern no matter what I did. I drank, used, ate, sniffed and was often miffed.

Food, alcohol, drugs, sensual pleasures--thank God I've transcended this level and there is no more lure.

It was horrible being a slave to food and alcohol--the conduit to the devil as I fell to lower levels.

I learned it was genetic--that my ancestors could NOT drink, not one atom or their lives were ruined.

If they didn't drink they became great famous orators but if they drank they sunk low to fruitless endeavors.

Alcohol's too easy man. The beer has 52 chemicals, it's cow piss and I was addicted to it/half German.

You take one drink and you have NO idea where you'll end up or what you'll say or do--could be the end of you.

See the impossibility of taking even one atom--it's a biochemical change by your mere decision.

How to live life without alcohol? If artistic/philosophical you may like a little herb, it's an opener not a blot.

NECESSARY DAY OF HUMILIATION

CHEAP SHOTS

What are flying monkeys? It's when they get their friends against you, used as an army to persuade/cajole.

Necessary phase of humiliation where no one knows who or what you are tho' you thought you were a star.

You gotta build back up that's all. Back on the potter's wheel--may take decades after the fall.

God abandons sinners to their own choices with a simultaneous loss of protection for the voiceless.

He abandoned me to my sin then I lost His hedge of protection and the evil world flowed in.

He did not abandon me to my own devices until I had first abandoned Him by my evil choices.

When God LET'S GO of a sinful society to it's own sinful freedoms all hell breaks loose in bedlam.

When this happens there's no restraining grace and sin runs rampant thru society in unending tragedies.

SEXUAL IMMORALITY INDICATES ABANDONMENT

The first indication of divine abandonment is sexual immorality. There is no control, it's just reality.

Massive uncontrollable sin is both the cause and result of God's abandonment/cessation of restraining grace.

When God abandons a tidal wave of sin flows in and it's a sudden happening after getting away with things.

When a society becomes immoral and pornographic, God's wrath is in effect.

When abandoned by God society operates in lusts of the heart--not constitutional restraint--and impurity.

CHEAP SHOTS

The heart is unrestrained then the body follows and you have a pornographic culture, horribly shallow.

Secondly, God gives em over to **DEGRADING** passions--we're going down into greater debauchery son.

Degrading passions defined: **GROSS** affections, **VILE** desires, **PERVERSION** and homo inversions.

Lesbianism/homosexuality is one example of exchanging the natural for the unnatural/inverting reality.

DEGRADING PASSIONS

Due to a mothering instinct women are usually the **LAST** to degrade--proof we're in the latter days.

The lesbian movement is vocal, loud, fierce and even violent. They wanna kill kids/I'm afraid of em.

Women denying their maternal instinct and going into reverse are most disgusting, I'd say the worst.

ALL virtue is gone when homosexuality invades the female gender and similarly the men sought each other.

Men with men--**BURNING** in their craving towards each other. Torches, kindling exploding in desire.

Sin has a **LURE**. This they misconstrue as truth--that they were **BORN** to be with the same sex, for sure.

One consequence of sinful choices is deadly diseases. It becomes unwholesome when lust never ceases.

When perversion becomes **THE** way of life and it's **APPROVED**/exalted it indicates God's wrath.

Thirdly, God gives em over to a depraved **MIND**. Heart is rotten, body follows then the mind **GOES**.

CHEAP SHOTS

What is a depraved mind? A mind tested and found USELESS, disqualified from it's intended purpose.

DEPRAVED MINDS

It's a nonfunctioning mind where reasoning is so corrupted, the intellect a crippled lunatic.

Intellectual faculties can't function when morality written in hearts is replaced by cultural immorality.

When conscience can't operate they naturally do things that are not proper-- embarrassing losers.

When mind is corrupted people don't think right. They don't seek old paths but advocate evil blights.

Along with unwholesomeness comes a depreciation of all the virtuous things of our past's loveliness.

Those who are worthy of death not only do the same but give hearty approval to those who practice them.

THO' THEY KNOW IT'S WRONG

They know it's wrong, they know the consequences but they give hearty approval anyway: that's sin.

When Bill Clinton was caught in his scandalous immorality his approval went UP--of course it did!

The awful sinners who love their sin feel comfortable with a leader who is like them. That's humanity son.

Without conscience, reason or restraint a society becomes like lustful gross beasts: a tragedy.

Running wild: It gets to the Jerry Springer level where things are so bizarre we're shocked then tired.

CHEAP SHOTS

Look at your society and ask yourself: Is this pornographic homosexual depravity or not?

The purveyors of this filth are the cultural icons we see everywhere. It's social hypnotism I declare.

The universities are hotbeds for the advocacy of this kind of iniquity so we must see them as our enemy.

The greatest indication of God's final wrath is a society who won't tolerate ANGER AGAINST SIN.

Any society that suppresses the truth in unrighteousness, condemning the light, indicates God's wrath.

We have five senses plus two spiritual senses: reason and morality which are so strong we can feel lost.

There's even a movement in modern churches to REMOVE the scripture but it's written in reason/heart.

LIVING LIFE AS HE WILT THE SPIRIT WILTS

Believing he can live his life any way he wants without consequence, he plunges downward fast.

They don't thank Him as the Source of everything they have--cuz their deeds are evil they stay bad.

They don't honor God cuz then they'd have to be accountable to Him for their beloved sins.

Sinners live with five major lies. The first is life is random--not something controlled if sin is despised.

If they go bad it's cuz someone else abused them, they weren't loved or lacked self-esteem.

He was "basically good" but with psychological problems from environmental failures--what liars!

CHEAP SHOTS

The bible is absolute truth. God is sovereign and **NOTHING** is random: it's good news for you.

Into this vacuous self-centeredness is sucked deeper darkness of useless, futile human ideas.

Their thinking became futile and their foolish heart was darkened. Romans 1: 21.

EMPTY, USELESS human ideas. Does this remind you of where we're at like with gender--are they serious?

Anosognosia: Their darkness is so profound they can't assess their true condition: proud morons.

When they don't see fit to acknowledge/thank God it's false religion: man at his lowest worshippin'

FALSE RELIGION IS THE LOWEST

The whole world is fanatically religious but paganism is still paganism and there's no way out but Jesus.

Man is not magically evolving up--ascending--to God but quite the opposite, that's how it goes y'all.

Man falls from the truth of God into the slime of religion. This is an automatic process as Satan is waitin'.

False religion is the Satanic counterfeit. In every church you go you must look for it: add-ons, skits.

Religion is not man's highest but man at his lowest. Not man finding God but Satan his evil host.

False religion has many complexities in it's Satanic system: high titles with robes and snubs.

Titles, robes, authority, influence and power of the deacon or elder: such is the hierarchy of fakers.

CHEAP SHOTS

These idols come in all forms: from primitive statues from the lowest cultures to Gods of self/sex/mother.

From pantheistic worship of the earth to eco-feminism then to Islam. It's all the same bag ma'am.

VISIBLE CYCLES IN HISTORY

These are visible cycles in history going on all the time. Before, now and in future man crosses the line.

I gave them over to the stubbornness of their heart to walk in their own devices. That was me twice.

If people would walk in My ways I would quickly subdue their enemies/punish their adversaries. God

I would turn from abandoning em to giving em victory over their enemies, forever defeated without cease.

The KEY? Listen to Me, walk in My ways. The only hope for this or any society: Hear My word and obey it.

Trump is so savvy because he's Daddy. He takes care of business because he's a genius.

Trump did excellently shutting down flights now he's gotta deploy troops to the border: shut it fast!

HEALTH: IT'S ABOUT LOOSE FLESH

It's about loose flesh. We all show signs of aging with time-- it's just a matter whether you can live with it.

V-8 juice, fruit, smoothies, guacamole, grapes, healthy candies, cheese, salmon: all easy on digestion.

It's called an "aged face"--who wants it? Well no worries, there's ways of getting around it, look it up.

CHEAP SHOTS

I'm entirely intellectual but also sensual what with music and all that...it's the combo of both ya' know.

Music instantly opens me to other worlds and it's always such a relief, I gotta do more of that to stay free.

Didn't know a thing at all, just fishing around, putting pressure on all hopin' somethin' would turn up.

"We never shoulda been married in the first place" yah but can't we always say that when mad at the ass?

ENGINEERED VIRUS

To President Trump: Please appoint Michael Savage and Mike Adams as our Coronavirus Czars Sir.

Liberals naturally trivialize coronavirus since that's how they handle everything. No facts/utopian vision.

They haven't even tested in America until March 2 [tomorrow] and the increase is EXPONENTIAL.

Viruses engineered: When they're real they cover em up but when not they hype em up to get power.

In fear of the coronavirus Chinese are escaping to our west coast. Due to city POOP, it's gonna spread fast.

Instead of telling em not to eat bat soup they tell em not to be xenophobic when they even eat bat POOP.

Progressive liberals are not concerned about a fatal virus spreading fast just mean words on the internet.

So it's ok to eat dogs--20 million a year in China--just cuz their culture does it? Cultural relativism STINKS!

Cure for sleep apnea/choking: breakfast-only plan. But most wanna eat/prefer that cumbersome mask.

CHEAP SHOTS

Caution with "cashmere blend". It could have polyester in it or other deadly modern fabrics--lethal/sickening.

OK I won't call you a bad driver just a "European" driver but that doesn't make it any easier for me dear.

It took me a lifetime to prioritize black cashmere cardigan vests which for office/house warmth are the best.

I'm enjoying panettoni [Italian fruit bread] in the morning then go light for brunch then nothing else.

Grape juice first [grapecure for cancer]. Then panettone [and what a morning] then just V8 juice later.

In this new diet lifestyle there are no need to wash dishes. Just live your delicious life as thou wishes.

STARCHIVORE-PESCATARIAN-FASTARIAN [ITALIAN]

Why do cats love panettone? Cuz it's filled with butter honey.

It's not what you eat but the reversals between em. Starch then later protein, fast 16 hours.

Starchivore-pesca-fastarian Italiana: Panettone breakfast, shrimp/salmon/tuna salad for brunch.

Panettone, banana bread, Mexican fruit breads: It seems every culture has em for our happy breakfasts.

CARB-UP in the morning with warm, sweet starchy/fruity pastry then LATER have a little fish Missy.

Fry or bake salmon. Saute shrimp in garlic butter. Make tuna salad with red onion/bell/olive/celery/oil.

That's two delicious meals and total hormonal reversals: starch breakfast, protein lunch, daily fast.

CHEAP SHOTS

One piece of delicious banana bread with butter sustains me until night. Then fish, just a bite.

With each food reversal between carbs and protein/fat it's like the body cures itself: it re-adapts.

What works marvelously better is elimination cuz nothing gets stopped up as the reversals keep it movin'.

If I feel a little sick I simply switch: to the other macronutrient, carbs vs. protein/fat.

Recall there are only three macronutrients: carbs, protein/ fat and the hormones evoked are radically different.

I'm no longer dieting to restrict macronutrients--carbs or fat--but to reverse between em as correctives.

IT'S EATING LIKE EUROPEANS

It's not what you eat as much as the reversals between em which kicks it into a new level correcting it all.

Most beautiful supermodel said "when I go to parties the first things I hit are the ice creams and cakes".

Eat as the Europeans do--they look a lot better than us. Banish all you know, eat your panettone then fast.

V-8 juice, panettone with butter. YUM. Slice cheese and a few grapes maybe later.

I got the panettone in the house and he can eat in his man shed when he wants--and he loves this freedom.

All processed food is largely soy, a cheap crop. It makes us all ugly and fat so switch to panettone ol' chap.

I believe it's the diet he gave me. Fruit, nuts, cheese, salmon for special and one meal a day.

Don't listen to anyone about your diet, even me. If it makes sense try it, it's worked like a charm for 33.

If it's made with soy can you really call it a "pizza" or dangerous crap from that cheap crop?

If you love pizza like I do make it with **CAPUTO** dough, it's soy-free or you'll look like the ordinary uglies.

SOY sounds healthy to most women who go in for anything seeming exotic, Asian or pagan.

Soy is an estrogen mimicker as boys get boobs and girls the monthly blues before ten, just look at em.

Food means mother. Something happened with that early broken bond and food was a constant problem.

BAD DRIVERS ARE SELFISH

Bad drivers see themselves as good drivers. Don't listen to that--does he follow too close/go too fast?

When he's following too close, does he also take his eyes off the road? **NEVER** go with him again girl.

When you've said you're scared to death, does he slow down or argue instead? Kick him outa your bed.

Nothing's worse than a car accident. You're amputated or end up in burn unit--think of this/don't forget it.

If you're afraid of someone's driving--even a spouse--do **NOT** get into the car again with that louse!

As I learned in Driver's Ed, a "good driver" is defined as having relaxed **RIDERS**. That's all that matters.

If you don't feel perfectly right and relaxed with someone's driving, **DO NOT GET INTO THE CAR** with em.

CHEAP SHOTS

Never speed up to please the guy behind. Who cares about him--never you mind.

NEVER BORED NOR LONELY

I'm never bored nor lonely. I've got so much to keep me busy due to my inner journey.

They are zombies here but they'll let you live your own life and be there in an emergency--what else is there?

Clothing companies call synthetic creep "making the fabric stronger" while it makes you sick forever.

100% wool . happy, warm, athletic, on the ball. 10% nylon in it for "strength": dizzy, acidic, sick as hell!

The contradiction is using SPANDEX [tight poison goes way in] for ATHLETICS [energy blocked, sickened].

Had shrimp fettuccini yesterday--it was so good I had it again today and overate: acidic, bloated, irate.

Rotate meals: what was good yesterday will turn on you today. Never over eat/don't eat twice in a day.

Curry is made up of anticaronaviral superfood spices. Combined with protein and veg = major detox.

Sweet starch in the morning--croissants or whatever--and shrimp in the aft: now be thin forever.

TEMPERAMENTAL DIGESTION

Digestion becomes so temperamental you learn to go easy or endure ruined days of physical agony.

Cuz once it's iN you, darn--what you gonna do? It's serious stuff what you put in, like all drugs.

CHEAP SHOTS

I drank too much V8 juice one day and suffered painful ACIDITY later--it delays then explodes in fever.

If I want happy predictable days, I gotta go REAL easy with the food. Everything planned, rotated, routined.

Most people have steel guts. They eat big dinners and not choke, they can eat anything and not go berserk.

My skinny grandma ended up on one meal a day. If she ever had two, her life would quickly degrade.

1: shrimp fettuccini 2: panettone 3: pizza, 4: guacamole 5: salmon 6: crab salad 7: grapes/olives/salsa.

Mine is a high-powered engine that's made to run on FAT and GLUCOSE and loves the COLD--ice cream?

LOVE your cats—don't get so many. In all groups it's best to constrain not add cuz less is more honey.

GOAL: FIND YOUR NICHE/WILL MAKE YA RICH

Your goal should be to find your NICHE. It is your highest possibility designed before birth and will make you rich.

Karen Kellock on Completion and the Creative Act

If each quip [two-liner] is a condensed chapter and there are 50 thousand quips in the Manual, it's a big one.

I wrote prolifically for ten years then realized other things had atrophied so I stopped, most profitably.

I've completed my work and now it's just home, home, HOME! Just my own situation: in SITU, ohm.

CHEAP SHOTS

I've written all I'm gonna write: 112 books on social psychology in a new theoretical light.

New projects: I'm gonna fall back to salsa trumpet before it atrophies and learn how to make panettone.

Not so much internet, perhaps an hour a day. I can't find anything interesting anymore anyway.

Gonna walk around the property for a change and look at the awesome view or the mountain ranges.

God starts things but He also stops them, I believe the writing has finally stopped after years: TEN.

God accomplishes great things on earth and He does it thru people: repentant, ready, apt to receive.

With completion of the Creative Act the discoverer returns to the child, a mere page not a King or Queen.

COMPLETION IS BACK TO CHILD

I just wanna be a child now, in the right-brain all the time. Retire into the infantile, mystical, psychotic!

I've finished writer's journey now I'm a child on a Saturday, running around and enjoying my property.

Gonna make a playlist of Downtempo Lounge Jazz for a week. Just found new goodies, high as a kite!

Many wonderful things now that I'm done with social psychology and all that stuff! God said "enough!"

Now that I don't have to write about crazy family systems and narcissists I can just enjoy new music!

Creative Act is a structure in nature [e.g. flower]: it has a beginning [inception] and an ending [completion].

CHEAP SHOTS

Whatever you focus on you screen **OUT** other things that could atrophy. Something to think about anyway.

I was a salsero trumpeter, I don't want that to atrophy. I will return to that, also painting what I see today.

Stop selling yourself and do something you can sell.

Stop taking back traitors. How quickly we forget the treasonous for they were soul-murderers.

Have the guts to **DRAW LINES** and boundaries. This takes strength but do it or things get quickly crazy.

People are cruel. Even little ol' ladies will misadvise you on new age principals then your life goes to hell.

You must draw lines with sinners demanding they repent or get lost--THIS is being boss.

TWO LIVES: PREPARATION AND SUCCESS

There are two lives: preparatory and success. The first is hellish, not just learning but overcoming messes.

You're into success mode now, the messes and horribleness is over--that was your war.

The war is over. You won't be suffering over narcissists anymore for you've got your **OWN** reality galore.

They were so friggin' cruel! But that was released from you being so weak. It was a system: lady/freak.

Merkel is the proprietor of the Kalergi Plan--to make the whole world brown, controllable and dumbed.

Being invaded was the biggest eye-opener and evoked viewpoints and talents of a major overcomer.

CHEAP SHOTS

Mass invasion evoked nationalism, and personal invasion evoked the True Self: what it wants and doesn't.

So I thank my invaders, you taught me more than a library of books. Thru you I learned about hooks/crooks.

Before being invaded I trusted everybody. I saw no differences and was a lunatic and crazy.

There is nothing more sickening than a justifier of strange and brutal customs under cultural relativism.

America thru the schools has so lost its way it can't even tell what is evil or good, it's what the others say.

How many legs does a dog have if you call his tail a leg? Four--calling a tail a leg doesn't make it so, ok?

I don't mind you copying me--I'm very evocative--but at least get it right, you mess it up day and night.

A LADY HAS GRACE AND INTELLIGENCE

A lady is intelligent, a good conversationalist, graceful and she will have an inner beauty. C.S. Lewis

All irksome memories are just a concept--remember that. You don't really know how it happened, so what.

Along with lack of self-discipline is under-estimation of the threat. Too casual and easy, not circumspect.

All 50,000 quips that went into the 112 Karen Kellock psychology books went on twitter first.

Bad stuff happens. We're tough, let's deal with it. Trump on Coronavirus readiness.

I was always hypersensitive so being with people was an assault on my SENSES/heart/mind so I'd get wild.

CHEAP SHOTS

Guard against external threats not let em in then lock us down thru Martial Law--it's unconstitutional.

Because of your multi-adaptations and overcoming revelations you now have much to give em.

SICK OF IT: I JUST WANT JESUS

A drag queen performs in bars for adults. There's a lot of sexual stuff going on and you allow it for kids?

It's the difference between a boy and a man. Brother you have nothing to offer me, I feel so less-than.

The world is filled with flying monkeys out to get you. If you don't draw lines they'll take your home too.

Women are now seeing the lost joys of just staying HOME. This is one good result of the virus panickin'

They'll worm their way into home then take over. Stand firm on boundaries in life style or whatever.

Way back then he was just a dashing imposer but when I saw him decades later he was a toothless loser.

The mere fact you listened to a lady who said to let em in anyway showed you still needed the lesson, ok?

Hate is heavy and it bonds you with the person. That's the reason for forgiveness or life is hell son.

When your time has come God will fill you with the right words. Don't worry or rehearse.

What do you take me for, just a loser without her own life--I'm supposed to lay down/let you take me over?

Take joy: the fact he stole money from you is the reason he's staying away. So it's worth it: hurray.

CHEAP SHOTS

She had an army against you--that's being "social". That's how women get the edge ya' know.

"It is the careless ease of self-confident fools that destroy them" is the most important verse to me, man.

When the enemy flourishes like a green olive tree just wait 'til he's mowed down like dead grass, see?

AVOID SELF-PROMOTION, YOU'RE ROTTEN

I hate how he promotes himself. Not so much the subject matter but him, him, HIM and I'm done with it.

Sorry, you showed disrespect in so many other ways too. That's a boy not a man--boys can't see one's value.

For who are YOU compared to God? A little humility would make you so much better, being flawed.

The saint writhes in remorse. Letting go of past faux pas is our major job, not acting like we're the best.

After being born again we're aware of our sin nature--a natural thing for man-- making us humbler.

I'm sick over the past. Paul's ONE goal was to let it go and proceed to what lies ahead, cuz it was so hard.

There's nothing to feel ego about, it was dear Jesus who pulled us outa the whole mess created by US.

You can be insane/wretched having never been taught right but it's still gotta be corrected, right?

Paradoxically, HUMILITY--being less--releases creative powers and we become the glorified best.

Coronaviris is the perfect excuse not to see people, let em in or conform to social expectations: be free.

CHEAP SHOTS

Yes the past taught me more than a library of books but it sure is hard to forget it for all the crooks/kooks.

MAJOR PROBLEM: NOT STANDING GROUND

My major problem when immature was not standing my ground and mal-adapting to em with addictions.

I see clearly what the framing set-up was--the system into which I was put--and my evolution waking up.

It hurt like hell being tormented by a buncha hicks when I didn't know any better about all their tricks.

They hurt me so much but I was in denial about it. It didn't illuminate scientifically till now, imagine that.

All the manipulative devices in human interaction I learned of in school I now experienced by the "cool".

I'm done listening to people talking. I just want MUSIC, MOVIES and looking out the window MUSING.

I'm done wasting time on political videos I'm not even listening to. Music, think, write: muse!

For the born again God works everything to their good since they are called by HIM.

No miracles, mysticism, making friends or magical and flashy spiritual gifts are necessary: just HIM.

P. S. Dog meat: you mean cuz some weird culture has a brutal custom we're supposed to accept it? Bullsh*t!

Caronavirus was globalism's last straw but it wasn't its rebirth it was its death: we want nations instead.

SELF-GLORIFICATION OR BE GLORIFIED?

CHEAP SHOTS

Forget self-glorification, we're rotten. But because of Him we can be glorified if first we repented.

In California I was invaded by a gang of boys and the police wouldn't protect me. Liberals, see?

These awful boys taught me more than a library of books: about psychology, developmental, schools.

They held me hostage in my own home knowing I had no protection and these lessons wrote these books.

My alcoholic husband at the time was a trojan horse linking to the outer evils, to my hurt.

Then he became a flying monkey for my sister destroying my reputation through constant calumny.

And there you have the sick system: interlocking jealousy patterns in a HYPER-social generation.

The concentric circles spread outward: Having been bashed we find others to finish/trash us.

Watch out for evil helpers. They can do you in better than anyone since they got a leg in and you're a dunce.

By GRACE you were saved and not of thyself--it was a gift of God. He saved me in spite of those flaws.

So how can any of us boast? But I did expend the energy to complete the Creative Act He put inside of me.

He took out ALL my enemies even while still in sin. As I look back it's HIM I'll be worshippin'.

CHEAP SHOTS by Karen Kellock Ph.D.

100 KAREN KELLOCK BOOKS

AFFINITY OR MISERY
AGELESS CORNUCOPIA
AMERICA AWAKE!
AMERICA'S DAFT ERA
ARTS OF PALEO FASTING
AUTOPHAGY ON CHEATERS
BACKSTABBING NEUROTICS
BETRAYAL TRAUMA
BOOMERS AND BROKENNESS
BOOT ON NECK
CHAMPION GUIDES
COMMIE NUTHOUSE
COMMIES
COMMUNIST SPIRIT
CONTAGION OF MADNESS
CONTAGIOUS MADNESS
CULTURE CLASH BASHED
DAFT LEFT
DAILY FASTARIAN
DAM RATS
DIVERSITY IS CRUELTY
E-RACE WHITE
EVIL FREAKS (Beyond Gross)
THE END OR A BEND?
FEMALE BULLIES AND FEMI-NAZIS
FEMALE CARNALITY
FEMALE DUMB DOWN
FEMALE POWER DRIVE
FEMINISM AND RUIN 1 & 2
FIX FOR MISFITS
FOOLS & TRAMPS
FREEDOM SPEAKING
FRENEMY ENABLER
FRENEMY LIAR
FRENEMY THIEF
FRENEMY TRAITOR
TRENEMY TYRANT
GENIUS IS HELD DOWN
GLOBALISLAM
GOD USES THE FLAWED
HAZE OF THE LATTER DAYS

THE HERD IN WORDS
HIX POLITIX
HOW THEY RUINED US
JUST SKIP DINNER
LE FEMME AND THE COMMUNIST SPIRIT
LIBERAL CHAOS & ROT
LIBERAL DOUBLETHINK
LIBERAL GALL 1 & 2
LIBERAL SHOVE-DOWNS
LOCK YOUR GATE
LOSERS and Femme Fatales
MANUAL FOR SUPERIOR MEN
MODERN ART FROM HELL
MOSTLY FAKE
NOTES TO CHAMPS 1 & 2
OVERCOME FRENEMIES
PC MAKES US CRAZY
PEOPLE ARE CRUEL
PEOPLE PROBLEMS 1 & 2
PERSECUTED GENIUIS
POLI-PSYCH MYSTERIES
PRETENTIOUS SLOBS
QUEEN BEE
RED NEW DEAL
RETURNING TO FIRST NATURE
SEASON OF TREASON
SEPARATE MEANS HOLY
SOCIAL HYPNOTISM
SOLITUDE SOLUTION
SUPERCILIOUS
THE SCHOOLS SCREWED EM UP
TOAD TO PRINCE
TRIALS CYCLES
TRUMP VS. GROUP
TRUST IN TRASH
THE TRUTH ABOUT PEOPLE
UNDERHEANDEDLY CLEVER
WALK TALL WITHIN WALLS
WE'RE NOT ALL ONE
WINNERS SKIP DINNER
WORK OR SMERK

AUTHOR BIO

Karen Kellock Ph.D.

Ph.D Political Psychology, UCI 1976
Post-Doctoral: UCI Medical School
Department of Psychiatry
Grants NIMH, NIAAA

Ph.D. dissertation "A Systems-Theoretic View of Pathologic Interaction" made an early mark as the "Wife of the Alcoholic Syndrome". Postdoctoral research at UCI Medical, Dept. of Psychiatry on the systems surrounding pathology on NIMH and NIAAA federal grants: *The Contagion of Madness: The Psychology of Neurotic Interaction and Pathological Systems*. Therapy tool Therapeutic Playwriting introduced the play *Mary and Murv: Gruesome Twosomes in the Alcoholic Marriage*. She taught Abnormal Psychology and Pathological Systems Theory at UC and CSU campuses and developed "the Debris Theory of Disease" in five books and website: (www.karenkellock.org): *Champion Guides, Daily Fastarian, Just Skip Dinner, Arts of Paleo Fasting, Ageless Cornucopia. Manual for Superior Men is a* pick-it-up-anywhere book that you can't put down (20,000 Kellockialisms) and ever on your desktop it should be found (or this Ebook for superior wordsearch of new jargon).